RETROSPECTIONS

BY

A. QUINN JONES, SR.

NOVEMBER 1967

Gainesville, Florida

ISBN: 1-4107-9777-5 (e-book)
ISBN: 1-4107-9776-7 (Paperback)

This book is printed on acid free paper.

1stBooks – rev. 11/03/03

TABLE OF CONTENTS

FOREWORD

Sunday, May 19, 1957, the Faculty and Students presented a program in the new high school auditorium honoring your humble servant in the cause of education on the verge of his retirement from Lincoln High School and the teaching profession after forty-two years of continuous service. To me this was a very touching occasion, filled with solemnity and traces of joy and satisfaction. An audience filled the auditorium to its capacity participated in this program. The audience stood and joined in singing, " Lead On, O King Eternal". After which, the Lincoln High School Chorus, directed by Mrs. Geraldine Y. Fields, sang "Let Us Now Praise Famous Men." I recall the most appropriate prayer by Rev. W. M. Ferguson, Pastor of Mount Pleasant Methodist Church. Dr. G. L. Porter, Executive Secretary of the Florida State Teachers' Association gave the occasion and brought greetings in behalf of this organization, also greetings from a representative of the Alachua County Board of Public Instruction, Wilford Griffin, President of the Lincoln High School Student Body and the President of the Alumni Association. "My Here " rendered by Miss Catherine Berry, Soprano and Mr. Julius Harper, Tenor followed with Presentations and closing with a song: "Let My Soul Rise in Song" by the Lincoln Chorus and Benediction by Reverend Leroy Tillman.

After the presentation of this program and during the course of conversations with Dr. Porter, he advanced the idea or suggestion that I should write some memoirs of my life experiences. I had never thought of writing anything about myself. My thinking was that it would appear somewhat egotistic. Again, Mr. Eric Roberts, sportswriter for the Pittsburgh Courier, visited Gainesville, his hometown at least once yearly and always visited me, and on every visit, he has mentioned to me that I should write about my activities. But the latest suggestion was made to me in October of 1967 by my wife, Mrs. Frederica M. Jones. Therefore, I decided reluctantly to write these Retrospections with the idea in mind that they might be somewhat of an incentive to those who might chance to read them and that they might reveal something of the sacrifice involved by one who sincerely desires an education along with the desire to render service thereafter. This treatise gives a brief autobiography, early training, and education including teaching activities of forty-two years, thirty-six of which were in Alachua County, Gainesville, Florida.

CHAPTER I

EARLY YEARS

In the Southern Section of Quincy, Florida known to its inhabitants at that time by the name, "Spring Hill", the writer was born on a two-acre tract of land including a small cottage which sheltered a family of seven children, Viz: Sarah J., Rosa Lee, Hester B., Simon Peter, Josephine, Allen Quinn, and Disney Theodore. The cottage in which we lived was comfortable and was equipped with the necessary conveniences of that era. It possessed two brick chimneys with fireplaces for burning wood and hard coal which were the principal fuels for heating. At a later date coal burning steel stoves were used in the homes for heating and ironing. Previously, irons were heated in the fireplace to do the ironing. The steel cooking range which burned wood, occupied a prominent place in the kitchen for cooking food for the family. Few foods were left over from day to day for there were not any means for preserving food as is being done by modern-day methods. Later ice boxes and containers which held factory manufactured ice were utilized in a limited manner to preserve foods. Water for the family's use was supplied from our thirty-foot piped well lined with pipe twelve inches in diameter with a cylindrical metal bucket attached to a rope and pulley for drawing the water therefrom. Later a metal force pump replaced the well for getting water.

The family washing was done in wood tubs used to contain water for that purpose. However, later the tin tub came into use.

My father led the family in daily prayer. My mother taught me the following prayer which I have never forgotten:

> "Now I lay me down to sleep, I pray the
> Lord my soul to keep
> If I should die before I wake, I pray the
> Lord my soul to take This I ask for Jesus
> sake. Amen"

The writer was the sixth child born March 3, 1893. My mother, Mrs. Rosa McDonald Jones and Father, Mr. Joseph Thomas

Jones informed me that I was baptized when an infant in Arnett Chapel A. M. E. Church, Quincy, Florida. All of my early years of church attendance and Christian experience occurred at this church and in June 1911, I confessed Christ as my savior and was received into full membership by the Pastor, Reverend F. R. Doyle. My church membership was transferred to Allen Chapel A. M. E. Church, Pensacola, Florida, October, 1916 where it remained until I moved to Gainesville, Florida, September, 1921, when I (we) became members of Bethel A. M. E. Church where it still remains to the present time.

To see snow fall and to roll snowballs out in front of our home on an early wintry morning was a phenomenon to me for this was during my pre-school days. Not since then have I experienced similar weather in Florida. The children in the family caught robins and other specie of birds that became disabled by the tremendously cold weather.

Some time during this spring, my parents talked about the Spanish-American War which was in progress. The Seaboard Air Line railroad was not more than a mile from where we lived. There was an occasion when the children were carried to the depot where we observed crowds of war recruits riding the train on their way to camp in preparation for fighting in the war with Spain.

I remember the first school I attended. It was located at the private home of Mrs. Annie Taylor and Miss Emma J. Wise, primary grade teachers. Because these two teachers were sisters, very kind, sympathetic, and motherly, I could never forget their love toward me and my admiration for them. They had such a great interest [in] us that I wanted to continue as one of my teachers after I had been promoted to a higher grade.

My elder sister, Sarah, taught me the English alphabets and the early beginnings to read. She was a teacher in Public School #1, at Quincy and taught me in two or three of the intermediate grades in this school. My sister was one of the three teachers, whose principal was Prof. C. A. Whitfield, a graduate of the state school, Tallahassee. My sister attended Atlanta University, Atlanta, Georgia during one term.

Reverend Mr. D. S. Selmore and Mr. A. F. Long were principals and taught me in the fifth and sixth grades respectively. The school term was six months.

It was during the principalship of Prof. George T. McDaniel that I completed grades seven and eight during two school terms. The school term was seven months. Mr. McDaniel was a recent graduate of the State Normal School (now Fla. A. and M. College) when he became principal. He recommended me and my friend and classmate, James A. Broston, to President Nathan B. Young for entrance to the first year high school class of the high school department of Fla. A. and M. College.

The Quincy Public School #I
A Simulated Drawing of the school I attended

The Quincy Public School was possibly about two miles from our home. It was necessary to cross a branch known as the " Ten-Yard Creek", between home and the school. When it rained real hard and long, it became almost impassable for one to cross the main stream on two logs about twelve feet long, placed together over the stream on which to walk. The water many times arose to a point above the logs. One can imagine how fearful we became if it should rain hard before school dismissed in the afternoon. My sister and I were small children and many times no one accompanied us back home from school. I am reminded of a boy, Tom Roby who rescued his sister who fell from the logs into the surging waters as she was carried down the stream. What an experience for young children.

Again, I recall the huge gorge about fifty feet deep and several hundred feet long that we had to pass on our way to and from school, unless we went the alternate longer route.

WORK EXPERIENCE

My mother's and father's tract of land adjoined the A. L. WILSON Company tobacco field. After school closed in the Spring of the year, I was employed by the manager of the tobacco farm to carry water to the workers -- keeping their thirst quenched throughout the five-day week period. I was eight years old. I was proud of this opportunity to earn some money to the extent that after school closed each year, employment awaited me to work at times in the tobacco barns and warehouses which extended over a period of several years. My wages increased each year as I became older. Some of my employers from time to time over the years until I completed my high school and college education were: A.L. WILSON Tobacco Company, Bruce Tobacco Company and American, Sumatra Tobacco Company.

I appreciated the opportunity to work and do something because my mother encouraged me to remain on the job, save the money that I would make to buy shoes, suits and other clothing in preparation for the opening of school each year. It was a glorious time for me each year when schools opened. There was another thing

5

that encouraged me greatly, viz: I was promised and given a suit by the supervisor, if I were a smart water-boy at the end of the tobacco season. Over these years, my wages ranged from $1.25 to $4.00 or $5.00 weekly.

My parents were not able to send me off from home to Tallahassee to school. However, because of their encouragement, I saved enough money to cover all of my school expenses through the first year of high school at the college. As a laundress, my mother could scarcely be surpassed in the quality of her work. My father was efficient as a gardener. Surprisingly, room, board, and laundry was eight dollars monthly for the term of eight months or $64.00. My brother Simon had completed a year at the college before my entrance which was quite an encouragement to me in making adjustments to a new environment. During those days, the distance from Quincy to Tallahassee was twenty-four miles by rail only. I had ridden on the train once the year before for the first tine. My going to Tallahassee this beginning school year was my second ride on a train. My older sister, Rosalee, entered Florida A. and M. the same year at the time that I entered but the term was incomplete by death in the College Hospital resulting from pneumonia. My brother, Simon, withdrew from Fla. A. and M. after completing the high school course at the close of my second year at the college. He worked for a year or more as a Pulman Train Porter before entering Meharry Medical College to study Dentistry in 1911, graduating June 1915 as a dentist. The writer graduated the same year from Florida A. and M. College with the Bachelor of Science Degree.

During my freshman, sophomore, junior and senior college years, my profoundest appreciation went to Dr. N. B. Young, President, who afforded work opportunity for me to take care of my school expenses throughout these years. I was employed as a table waiter, and an assistant in food service to both students and special table waiter for the teachers. During the last two years in college, my entire expense including room and board were taken care through the work performed. Summer vacations found me returning home to a job in tobacco barns and factory and the money earned therefrom took care of all incidentals including books and other materials that were needed. Thanks to a mother and father, although they were not financially able to support me in going through college, they gave me the maximum amount of encouragement to save money earned to help myself.

My brother, Simon, attending Meharry Medical College, at the same time that I was attending Fla. A. and M. would write me frequent letters of encouragement to persevere and remain in school. My sister, Sarah, although busy on the job as a teacher, found time to write letters of encouragement. She and my sister, Hester, not only wrote encouraging letters but also included in them, frequently, stamps and some other needed money. A quarter at that time, had the buying power of more than a dollar today.

OTHER COLLEGE EXPERIENCES

One experience was striking to me at the beginning of the first semester of the first year at the college in October when all the football aspirants for the varsity team were required to run two miles on the campus before the morning, practice. Many of the boys fell out on the run. I practiced but I did not make the team. Weight was against me. The faculty coaches included Dean G. M. Sampson were enthusiastic.

Over the years, I was a member of the Fla. A. and M. College Chapter of the Y. M. C. A. The membership fee was twenty-five cents a year. The Philomathean Literary Society whose membership included all students of college status, met bi-monthly and rendered programs.

The College Wits Club whose founder and organizer, Prof. E. B. Jones, composed of college men, was a very active campus organization. The club colors were black and gold, the forerunner of the Alpha Phi Alpha Fraternity which had been organized and founded at Cornell University in 1906. It was against the policy of the college to permit fraternities and sororities. The writer was one of the first presidents of this club.

The following is quoted from The College Arms monthly publication March 1915:

> "Reflection reveals the fact that after taking everything under consideration, Mr. Jones as President, has done more work with the Wits than any other president. He has succeeded in having more meetings and went as far as having the "Wits" give a program in public which the "Arms" hopes will be repeated every year."

1914 and 1915 School Term

Members of the Philomathead Debating Society

Essie Robinson	Althea Nixon
James Reddick	James Armstrong
Samuel Daniels	Oscar Lynch
Quinn Jones	Walter Hilyard
N.B. Young, Jr.	Ella Childs
Irma Archer	Nellie Raulds
Georgietta Mattox	Robert P. Stewart
Alma Rambo	Norton Roberts
Julia Eaverly	Lorenxa Richardson
William Golden	Lesesne Howard
E.E. Broughton	Marie Thomas
Sadye Hunter	Estelle Bellamy
Catherine Gardner	Grace Myers
Frank Taylor	Olive McCoy
James Dixon	Petrona Bonner
Albertina Edmonson	Maude Norton
L. W. Black	Mattie Lewis
Maggie Baker	Samuel Holly
Helen Chandler	Marion McCall
Fred Martin	Victor Postelle
Emma Dawson	Horace D. Goode
Eva Myers	Benjamin Crutcher

TUCKER HALL --- ANNEX

The room in which I lived was typical of all the dormitory rooms on the College campus. There were three cots in my room during my first year. Three boys occupied the room including myself. There was a closet in which to hang our clothing with a curtain at the entrance. A wash stand on which was the water pitcher and wash bowl, a soap dish, a rack to hang towels and wash cloths were there. There was a mirror in the room. The mattress on the bed was filled with cured rye grass which was sufficient for the term. One had to supply his own bedding. There was a wood heater in each room. The boys had to go to the wood yard to get their wood for heating purposes. Electric light drop cord from the ceiling of the room furnished light. This cord included a light bulb. There was a window in each room unless it was a corner room. Bath shower facilities with hot and cold water were located in the bath house between the two dormitories, viz: Tucker Hall and Tucker Annex.

When I completed high school and entered the college department, the college men were located near the North East entrance to the college campus in the "The College Men's Cottage." The surroundings were a little more improved and made us feel more distinctive for we were more on our honor. Our rooms were kept in order daily for they were inspected by a student representative from the Dean of Men's Department.

BOYS' DORMATORY ------ 1915

CARNEGIE   LIBRARY

Girls' Dormitory, Assembly Chapel, and Dining

Choir ----------1915

CADET MILITARY ORGANIZATION

The young men of the college were organized into three cadet military companies, in charge of a teacher commandant, Major W. H. A. Howard. Each company was commanded by a cadet captain and his fall complement of cadet officers selected from those students who had most exemplary conduct and soldery bearing. I attained the rank of second sergeant during high school. College students were exempted from duty and military drills. Worthwhile traits of neatness, punctuality, obedience, and healthy, manly bearing, a high regard for law and order were engendered among the students. A course of military calisthenics or gymnastics was given in the open air. A band composed of young men of all departments using twenty instruments formed the military band. I recall having had music instruction in playing the cornet, under Mr. Quintia Adderly. The student officers under the commandant assisted in maintaining discipline among the men students. They also assisted the college administration in the enforcement of campus and dormitory regulations -- orderly well kept rooms, corridors, wholesome and sanitary environment. Committees or groups of young men assumed weekly turns in the care of dormitory corridors, etc.

SOCIALS

Socials for the students were held monthly on the lawn of the girls dormitory, Gibbs Hall. Young men were permitted to go to the dormitory and ask to escort his girlfriend out on the campus for one hour which was allotted to them by the Dean of Girls. Only girls that were seventeen years old or older were permitted to participate in this social hour. Young men were permitted to escort their girlfriends to football games which were played on Saturdays in the afternoon. Likewise, the same was true of baseball. Fla. A. and M. and Tuskegee Institute baseball games stimulated a great amount of college spirit and enthusiasm. I enjoyed playing tennis at times during weekend leisure hours.

CULTURAL PROGRAMS

There were programs given of a cultural nature during the seven years that I attended Fla. A. and M. The following lectures or sermons were given during my senior year:

October 22, 1914	--	Rev. A. A. Hewett, Rector Episcopal Church, Tallahassee, Florida....Sermon
October 30	--	History and Development of Human Adornment—Miss R. O. Paige, Instructor of Dress Making and Millinery
November 4	--	Recital – Mrs. Martha Bradus Anderson, Soloist Miss Cleo Mae Dickerson, Pianist .....Chicago
November 8	--	Sermon: Rev. John A. Gregg, President of Edward Waters College, Jacksonville, Florida
December 22	--	Lecture: The Challenge of Socialism, Prof. John F. Matheus, Assistant Professor of Latin and English
January 1, 1915	--	Emancipation Address – Mr. S. H. Archer, Professor of Mathematics, Morehouse College, Atlanta, Ga.
January 7	--	Lecture: Hon. W.A. McRae, Commissioner of Agriculture State of Florida, Tallahassee
January 24	--	Sermon: Rev. Samuel Owens, Florida Baptist Institute, Live Oak
January 15	--	Lecture: Mr. W. H. Tobias, International Secretary of Y. M. C. A.
February 19	--	Lecture: The Negro Fifty Years Hence, Dr. M. W. Gilbert, President of Selma University, Alabama
February 16	--	Lecture: Dr. Brewer, Dean of Theology, Talladega College, Talladega, Alabama
February 21, 1915	--	Sermon: Rev. S. H. Barnwell, Thomsville, Georgia
February 22	--	Lecture: Sights and Scenes in the Old World, Rev. H. H. Proctor, Atlanta, Georgia
March 6	--	Lecture: Prohibition, Dr. Ira Landreth, Flying

		Squadron, Nashville, Tenn.
March 14	--	Sermon: Rev. J. A. Brown, Bethel A. M. E. Church Tallahassee, Fla.
March 24	--	Lecture: Mrs. Carrie Steele, Social Worker, Chattanooga, Tenn.
March 31	--	Lecture: Dr. Lymen, Secretary International Sunday School Association, Chicago, Illinois
April 9, 10	--	Lecture: Miss Josephine Pinyon, International Secretary of Y.W.C.A.
April 11	--	Sermon: Mr. J. G. Riley, Principal of Lincoln High School, Tallahassee, Fla.
April 16	--	Lecture: Dr. Oscar Dowling, President of Louisiana State Board of Health.

The writer was a character in several Shakespearian plays given during my junior and senior college years, viz: King Henry VIII, Macbeth.

Opportunity was afforded high school students to appear periodically on programs to which the public was invited. It was quite an experience for me in my first appearance to give a declamation entitled the "Tongue and the Sword." My English teacher, Miss Helen James, did an excellent job in training a country boy for a program of this kind, She was very sympathetic and patient with me. I had appeared before this on programs and plays in our public school but it seemed that my appearance or participation at Florida, A. and M. was different for my complex was that the audience would be more critical. However, I survived the shock.

On another program which I regarded important was my appearance on the Senior Class Day exercise in which I gave the Class Day Oration on the subject, "Abraham Lincoln."

At another time during my college days, I was privileged to have witnessed a renowned violinist, the Grandson of Frederick Douglass. Another program featured an outstanding soprano recital by Mesdame Hackley. Also one by Mesdame Denby, and a baratone recital by Saxton Whaley, a graduate of Florida A, and Y. College were superb.

Sundays were just as busy with activities as the week days. Noon day or mid-day chapel for devotion was attended by all students while Sunday School followed by the regular eleven o'clock service was a "Must." It was inspiring first of all to hear a message by Dr. N. B. Young and Prof. E. B. Jones and at other times by other members of the faculty or a visiting speaker. Weekly prayer meetings and devotionals were held under the auspices of the Y. M. C. A.

It was during the 1914-1915 school term that Booker T. Washington, the founder and President of Tuskegee Institute made an historical appearance at the college when touring the South fulfilling speaking engagements in several cities in Florida. President Young called a special college assembly to honor and receive him and his large delegation. This was the first opportunity afforded most of the students to see and hear this distinguished educator speak. I regarded this as being one rare occasion in my school career.

My college class in Geology, under Prof. L. E. Graves, made trips to Lake Jackson about three or four miles from the college campus, where we traversed parts of the lake to discover its depth, its habitat, the nature of the soil, its probable origin, source of water supply and its extent. It was novel for some of us since it was the first experience riding in [a] row boat.

There were times when my class in Astronomy studied the surface of the moon through the telescope during evenings when the moon was visible.

Our instructor in Trigonometry taught me how to use the transit or the Surveyor's instrument. There was one assignment given me by my instructor, Prof. F. C. Johnson that I shall never forget. I was required to draw a "Pipe Wrench Yoke", in [a] mechanical drawing. I preserved this drawing for a long time for it was basic to many other more difficult drawings. My free hand drawings were numerous.

15

HIGH SCHOOL COURSES COMPLETED

1908-9 - First Year –	1909-10 - Second Year -	1910-11 - Third Year -
English Algebra Latin Tailoring	English History Latin Grammar Plane Geometry Botany Drawing Tailoring	Latin (Cicero) Solid Geometry Physics Mechanical Drawing Tailoring

COLLEGE COURSES COMPLETED

1911-12 - Freshman-	1912-13 - Sophomore -	1913-14 - Junior -
English College Algebra Latin (Virgil) Biology	English (Argumentation) Trigonometry Chemistry Latin Epodes of Horace Current Events	Modern History Chemistry Geology Astronomy German

1914-15
- Senior –

Psychology Analytical Geometry	Advanced Physics Chemistry Economics

BACCALAUREATE SERVICE
May 23, 1915

Prelude ....Orchestra
Processional
Coronation
Invocation and Gloria
Anthem -- "Sons of Freedom" (Mundy).............................Choir
Scripture Lesson
Prayer and Response
Anthem -- "Ethiopia" (Mundy) ....Choir
Baccalaureate Sermon ....Rev. E. R.
Carter, Atlanta, Ga.
Solo..Miss   Ella
Childs
Doxology
Benediction
Recessional

COMMENCEMENT DAY EXERCISES
May 27, 1915

Processional
College Song...School
Invocation
Chorus -- "Morning"...Choral
Union
Baccalaureate Address.......................................Dr.   C.   V.
Roman, of
                          Meharry Medical College, Nashville, Tenn,
Chorus -- "A Perfect Day" (Bonds)....................................Choral
Union
Presentation of Diplomas and Conferring Degrees
Chorus -- Jubilee Songs
(a)
(b)
(c)

A. Quinn Jones, Sr.

God Be With You ....School

CLASS ROLL

Estelle Beatrice Bellamy, B.S.
        Ocala, Florida
Allen Quinn Jones, B.S.
        Quincy, Florida
Nathan Benjamin Young, Jr., B. S.
        Tallahassee, Fla.

ENGLISH NORMAL CLASS

Petrona Cadace Bonner
        Ocala, Florida
Ella Inez Childs
        Gainesville, Florida
Mattie Evangeline Lewis
        Tallahassee, Florida
Addie Blanche Masch
        Pablo Beach, Florida
Olive Augustia McCoy
        Fruitland Park, Florida
Grace Elizabeth Myers
        Sanford, Florida
Maude Mable Norton
        Tampa, Florida
Victor Leroy Postelle
        Lake Park, Georgia
Claudine Louise Taylor
        Tallahassee, Florida
Marie Margarette Thomas
        Orlando, Florida
Ida Salina Wiggins
        Roy, Florida

****

College Class Motto: "Finis Nondum Est"
Class Colors: Blue and Maize; Flower – Violet

****

English Normal Class Motto: "Upward and On."
Class Colors: Crimson and Gray; Flower – American Beauty Rose

****

COLLEGE CLASS OFFICERS

A. Quinn Jones, President
N. B. Young, Jr., Secretary
Estelle B. Bellamy, Treasurer

ENGLISH NORMAL CLASS OFFICERS

Victor L. Postelle, President
Maude M. Norton, Secretary
Olive A. McCoy, Treasurer

By referring to the outline of courses and curricula that I pursued toward graduation, were strictly academic. It is interesting to me when I compare the marking system used then based on the scale 50 to 100 and the system of letters used ten years later which were based on the letter, A, B, C, D, or F (fail). The mark 60 to 100 were passing grades, while 50 to 59 percent were conditional passing marks.

There was quite a contrast in my graduation from college in 1915 and that of the present time, fifty-two years afterward.

I rented a used cap and gown for graduation ceremonies for less than two dollars. I did not have the money to buy new shoes and other accessories for graduation as is done for and by members of graduating classes today. I ordered five invitations for graduation. I kept one invitation for my record and sent the other four home to mother and father and other members of the family. The one invitation is in possession of the writer after these many years in a scrap book. Along with this one invitation, it is also interesting to observe my individual graduation picture in cap and gown and a class picture.

In order to qualify for teaching in Florida schools, applicants were required to take the State Uniform Teachers Examination and secure a first, second or third grade teacher's certificate. I had taken the examination June 1913, two years before graduating from college, made a third grade certificate good for two years but was never used.

June following my graduation, I secured by examination a second grade teacher's certificate valid for three years.

Since the writer graduated from the Florida A. and M. College June 1915, indicates that he made satisfactory grades or marks throughout his school career at the college. I am reluctant to relate whether there was anything outstanding in his college career or not. However, the F.A.M.C. General Alumni Association at the commencement exercise presented him an award of ten dollars in gold for maintaining the highest scholarship among the graduates or the ranking student graduate. I had a profound appreciation for this worthy prize because at the moment, I was undecided where I would get ten dollars to pay the purchase price for my diploma and having it signed and executed by President N. B. Young and Dean John C. Wright. I gave the gold coin I had just received to have the diploma executed.

I received two other graduation gifts which I appreciated immeasurably: one a small pocket-size new testament Bible from the teachers whom I served meals daily in the dining room, and the other a booklet of choice quotations by Booker T. Washington from Miss M. E. Melvin, Dean of Women. I read selections from the Holy Scripture from this bible for many years to the children in school assemblies. The favorite selection was the thirteenth chapter of First Corinthians.

I quote the first and the last Daily Resolve from the Booker T. Washington Booklet:

Resolve to live up to the high water mark of daily duty. Whoever does this will meet with constant and unexpected happiness and encouragement.

Resolve daily to realize that the surest way to lift up ourselves is to lift up someone else.

A. Quinn Jones, Sr.

TABLE
YEARS OF TEACHING EXPERIENCE

No.	YEAR	MONTHS	SCHOOLS AND POSITION	COUNTY & NO. OF TEACHERS	GRADES IN SCHOOL	GROSS SALARY
1	1915	July, Aug., Sept.	Sawdust School Prin., Teacher	Gadsden 1 Teacher	1 to 8	$66.00
	1916	Oct., Nov., Dec., January	Pri., Teacher Marianna School	5 Teachers	1 to 10	$100.00
2	1916	July, Aug.	Sawdust School	Gadsden 1 Teacher	1 to 8	$44.00
	1917	Sept., Oct, Nov., Dec., Jan., Feb., March	Prin. of School # 44 Pensacola	Escambia 5 Teachers	1 to 4	315.00
3	1917	July, Aug. & Sept.	Roy, Florida Prin., Teacher Grades 7,8,9	Liberty Co. 4 Teachers	1 to 9	$75.00
	1918	Oct., Nov., Dec., Jan., Feb., & March	Roy, Florida Prin., Teacher Grades 7,8,9 Prin., Teacher School # 44 Pensacola	5 Teachers	1 to 4	315.00
4	1918 1919	Oct., Nov., Dec., Jan., Feb., Mar., April & May	Prin., Teacher High Sch. # 3 Pensacola	Escambia Co. 9 Teachers Taught: Eng., Math., Sci.	5 to 12	$680.00
5	1919 1920	Oct., Nov., Dec., Jan., Feb., Mar., April & May	Teaching Prin. High Sch. # 3, Pensacola	Escambia Co. 9 Teachers Taught: Eng., Math., Sci.	5 to 12	680.00
6	1920 1921	Oct., Nov., Dec., Jan., Feb., Mar., April & May	Assist. Prin. Washington H.S. # 3, Pensacola	Escambia Co. Nine Teachers Taught: Eng., Math., Sci.	5 to 12	720.00
7	1921 1922	8 Months	Union Academy Gainesville, Fla. Teaching-Principal Taught: Latin, Math., Science	Alachua County 11 Teachers	1 to 9	$1,000.00
8	1922 1923	8 Months 8 Months	Union Academy Gainesville, Fla. Teaching-Prin. Taught: Latin, Math. Science	Alachua County 11 Teachers	1 to 9	$1,000.00
	1923	June, July, August	Teaching-Princ. Arredonda School Taught: Grades 5 to 8	Alachua County 3 Teachers	1 to 8	$180.00
9	1923 1924	8 Months	Principal of Lincoln High School	Alachua County Gainesville	1 to 11	$1,160.00

No.	YEAR	MONTHS	SCHOOLS AND POSITION	COUNTY & NO. OF TEACHERS	GRADES IN SCHOOL	GROSS SALARY
			Taught: Latin, Math., Science			
10	1924	June, July, August	Prin., Teacher Arredonda School Taught: Grades 5 to 8	Alachua County 3 Teachers	1 to 8	$180.00
	1925	8 Months	Principal of Lincoln High School Taught: Latin, Math., Science	Alachua County. Gainesville	1 to 12	$1,200.00
11	1925 1926	8 Months	Principal of Lincoln High School Taught: Latin, Math., Science	Alachua County Gainesville	1 to 12	$1,200.00
12	1926 1927	8 Months	Principal of Lincoln High School Taught: Latin, Math., Science.	Alachua County Gainesville	1 to 12	$1,200.00
13	1927-	July, August, June	Arredonda School Prin., Teacher Taught: Grades 5 to 8	Alachua County 3 Teachers	Grades 1 to 8	$195.00
	1928	8 Months	Principal of Lincoln High School Taught: Latin, Math., Science	Alachua County Gainesville	Grades 1 to 12	$1,120.00
14	1928-	June, July, August	Arredonda School Prin., Teacher Taught: Grades 5 to 8	Alachua County Gainesville	1 to 8	$195.00
	1929	8 Months	Prin. of Lincoln High School Taught: Latin, Math., Science	Alachua County, Gainesville	1 to 12	$1,120.00
15	1929- 30	8 Months	Lincoln H.S. Principal Latin, Math, Eng., Science	Grades in School: Alachua County	1-12	$1,240.00
16	1930- 31	8 Months	Principal Taught: Math.	Alachua County	1 to 12	$1,160.00
17	1931- 32	8 Months	Principal Taught: Math.	Alachua County	1 to 12	$1,160.00
18	1932- 33	8 Months	Principal Taught: Latin	Alachua County	1 to 12	$800.00
19	1933- 34	8 Months	Latin	Alachua	1 to 12	$800.00
20	1934- 35	8	Latin	Alachua	1 to 12	$800.00
21	1935-	8	Latin	Alachua	1 to 12	$1,000.00

A. Quinn Jones, Sr.

No.	YEAR	MONTHS	SCHOOLS AND POSITION	COUNTY & NO. OF TEACHERS	GRADES IN SCHOOL	GROSS SALARY
	36					
22	1936-37	8	Latin & Gen. Sc.	Alachua	1 to 12	$1,250.00
23	1937-38	8	Gen. Science	Alachua	1 to 12	$1,250.00
24	1938-39	8	Gen. Science	Alachua	1 to 12	$1,275.00
25	1939-40	8	Lincoln Principal Taught: Science		1 to 12	$1,250.00
26	1940-41	8	Lincoln Prin. Taught: Eng. 12 Science 9		1 to 12	$1,250.00
27	1941-42	8	Lincoln Prin. Taught: Sc. 9 Eng. 12		1 to 12	$1,350.00
28	1942-43	8	Lincoln Prin. Taught: None		1 to 12	$1,500.00
29	1943-44	9	Lincoln Prin. Taught: None		1 to 12	$1,650.00
30	1944-45	9	Lincoln Prin. Taught: None		1 to 12	$1,650.00
31	1945-46	9	Lincoln Prin. Taught: None		1 to 12	$2,000.00
32	1946-47	9	Lincoln Prin. Taught: None		1 to 12	$2,250.00
33	1947-48	10	Lincoln Prin. Taught: None		1 to 12	$3,600.00
34	1948-49	12	Lincoln Prin. Taught: None		1 to 12	$3,800.00
35	1949-50	12	Lincoln Prin. Taught: None		1 to 12	$4,000.00
36	1950-51	12	Lincoln Prin. Taught: None		1 to 12	$4,000.00
37	1951-52	12	Lincoln Prin. Taught: None		1 to 12	$4,200.00
38	1952-53	12	Lincoln Prin. Taught: None		1 to 12	$4,560.00
39	1953-54	12	Lincoln Prin. Taught: None		1 to 12	$6,000.00
40	1954-55	12	Lincoln Prin. Taught: None		1 to 12	$6,185.00
41	1955-56	12	Lincoln Prin. Taught: None		1 to 12	$6,385.00
42	1956-57	12	Lincoln Prin. Taught: None		7 to 12	$6,585.00

Read Table Thus: The first year, 1915-16 teaching was done at the Sawdust one-teacher school in Gadsden County, grades 1 to 8, and Principal-teacher of the Marianna School, five teachers, grades 1 to 10 at a gross salary of $66 and $100.

Taught during the months of July, August, September, October, November, December, January.

CHAPTER II

TEACHING IMMEDIATELY AFTER GRADUATION

My first teaching experience and school employment following graduation May 27, 1915 was done July, August, and September in the one-room school "Sawdust" in Gadsden County. It was located a distance of about seven or nine miles from Quincy. My gross annual salary was $66. School classes were held in the Negro church in this community. It required about two hours by horse and wagon or buggy from Quincy to reach the school. I was housed and boarded at the home of Mr. and Mrs. Goodson who were progressive farmers and also parents of the school. My room and board was five dollars a month. My stay with them was most enjoyable for opportunity was afforded me to ride horses which they owned for farming and at times riding in wagon on weekend trips back home to Quincy. The Goodsons' produced a diversity of farm crops including the cultivation of tobacco. They produced about everything that any farmer did during that period: poultry, turkeys, pork, cattle, dairy products, truck farming as well as staple farm products.

Picture one teaching children entering the first grade or school for the first time along with a total number of twenty-five children in grades one up through grade eight all seated in a one-room church building without desks on which to write or place their books. The school day began at 8:30 A. M. with a ten-minute recess before noon. A noon period of one hour and closing the day at 3:00 P.M. Brief devotional periods were held daily including the singing of familiar songs, reading scripture selections from the Bible without any comment to comply with the school law. Friday afternoon periods near the end of the day, literary programs of some kind were given, involving songs, recitations, spelling matches, etc.

The school curriculum consisted of handwriting, reading in the first, second, third, fourth, fifth, on up through the eighth grade. Pupils were taught from the Baldwin Series of Readers. Spelling was taught. Primary children were taught numbers while children in grades four to eight were taught arithmetic from the Milnes' series of arithmetic textbooks. Geography, history, hygiene and physiology

were taught the upper grammar grade pupils from the adopted
textbooks in use at that time. Many of the children's parent were not
able to buy books for their children since free textbooks were not
furnished. One inadequate wood blackboard supplied for use.
Dimes, nickels and pennies were collected from the children to buy
white chalk for blackboard use. There were no brooms for sweeping
the church daily after school but instead of brooms the green foliage
from a wild weed which grew out around the church in the woods or
forest were collected and used to sweep the church. Children brought
their lunches with them from their homes in buckets and paper bags.
A water bucket and dipper were supplied for drinking water. Each
child brought his glass or drinking cup with him for his individual use
in getting water. There was no source of water on the grounds,
however, water was supplied from the home of Mr. and Mrs.
Goodson not too far from the church. There were separate outdoor
privies for boys and girls. To comply with the state school laws, the
county board of public instruction permitted communities where
schools were located to elect from their local citizens some man to
serve as supervisor of the school. It was through him that the county
superintendent of public instruction communicated with the parents of
the school community. Again, the law provided for the election of
trustees to serve or have general oversight of school property in each
school district in the county if the county owned any school building
or other school property. The county owned very little property
during those years.

At the close of this three-month school term, I was appointed
as a teacher-principal of the city public school at Marianna, Florida,
the county site of Jackson County. This was a five-teacher school
including the principal which was housed in a dilapidated school
building containing rough home-made desks, very little play space,
out-of-doors water pump for water supply, separate outdoor toilets for
boys and girls. The building was heated during cold weather by
means of wood heaters. Pupils supplied their individual drinking cups
or glasses for drinking water supplied in two or three gallon tin
buckets with a dipper in each of the five rooms.

Pennies, nickels and dimes were collected from the children to
buy chalk for the black board, for purchasing brooms for sweeping

the floor, and buying wood fuel for the heaters. A water pump was located on the grounds.

The teaching load was as follows: one teacher taught first and second grades; a second teacher taught third and fourth grades; a third teacher taught fourth and fifth grades; a fourth teacher taught fifth and sixth grades; and the principal taught eighth, ninth or tenth grade pupils.

The subjects taught in this school were about the same as those taught in the previous school. The daily, weekly, and monthly activities were also similar. Monthly report cards were given pupils to indicate their progress; however, there was not sufficient progress to warrant or justify graduation exercises.

The deportment and general conduct of children were far superior to that of children today. The school laws of Florida at that time permitted corporal punishment for pupil's improper conduct but it was to be reasonable. I did not experience grave cases of pupil bad behavior.

However, the minor cases were adjusted by reprimands and other means and measures at the school, viz: retention after school hours, reports to parents, suspension from school up to five days were permissible for serious cases of misconduct.

It was my ambition to continue to further improve my education after graduating from college. My classmate, Nathan B. Young, Jr., was given the opportunity by his father, Dr. Nathan B. Young, President to enter immediately the Yale University School of Law where he graduated with the LL.B. degree three years later in 1918. He immediately began the practice of law in St, Louis, Mo. where he resides to this date.

Lack of financial support retarded me in my desire to study to become a Doctor of Medicine at Meharry Medical College, hence I continued in the field of education.

Through Extension Study, I was awarded the M. A. Degree in the year 1920 from Oskaloosa College, Iowa, in the field of English, Psychology and Philosophy.

When I was principal of the Marianna School, I became a member of NAACP and was recommended by Dr. N.B. Young, President of Fla. A. and M. College, to the National office to become the agent of the Crisis, the official monthly magazine published by the NAACP. I served a small number of subscribers to the magazine in the Marianna area. I continued to renew my membership in this organization when I changed my teaching service to Pensacola, Florida. This city boasted a strong chapter of the NAACP at that time and through the invitation of this local chapter, the Negro community was honored by the visit and the address of Dr. W. E. B. Dubois, the Editor of the Crisis Magazine, and the Executive Secretary of the Association from the home office in New York City.

I was secretary of the Southern Protective Association, organized by Reverend C. A. Whitfield, pastor of Allen Chapel A. M. E. Church and the president, This was a city-wide general welfare organization. This was during World War I, when the community was experiencing many pathological conditions, racial and otherwise that needed the attention of the organization. I was not given any financial consideration for my service as secretary, but I remember there was the sentiment of some of the members of this organization to want to do something as a gesture of appreciation for my service. Hence, a motion was made and carried to the effect that this body donate to me $50.00 to help me attend University of Chicago Summer school during the approaching Summer quarter of 1919. I appreciated this donation, however, I could not supplement this amount with sufficient funds to follow through with going to summer school as badly as I desired to attend.

The Summer of 1916 lured me back to the Sawdust School for two months service and in the meantime, I was appointed as principal and teacher of School 44, Pensacola, Florida where I served during the regular 1916-17 winter term for another seven months from September through the month of March.

The chart further reveals that I was principal-teacher of the Public School at Roy, Florida during July and August, after which, I returned to Pensacola where I continued to serve for seven more months at School 44 from October through the month of April, 1917-1918.

It might be of interest to state that my sister, Mrs. Sarah J. Bennett, who lived in Liberty county and had been there for several years, along with Miss Ida Wiggins, a native of the town and a recent graduate and classmate of mine, were my assistant teachers.

Teachers like the children and their parents are always eager for vacation days to end and schools to open for their children. Possibly it is more peaceful at home when the children are absent for several hours daily. Furthermore, teachers must be able to live or have a livelihood. Incidentally, Negro teachers received less salary than white teachers and Negro children shorter school terms than white children. This situation changed during the fifties.

There are several important anniversaries in the life of an individual and marriage is one of them. During my tenure as principal-teacher of School 44, Pensacola, Florida, which had a faculty of five teachers including the principal, one of whom taught a class of primary children and served as the pianist for the school for all occasions. She demonstrated her ability as a teacher and was recognized as one of the better teachers of Escambia County, at that time she also served in the community as the Pianist of the Zion A. M. E. Church. This teacher was Miss Agnes Marion Smith. On January 2, 1918, we were joined in wedlock and her name changed to Mrs. Agnes Marion Jones.

She was not only musical but she possessed an unusual talent and training as an elocutionist, having been trained under Mesdame DesVerney. She played leading roles in Shakespearian plays during Summer school at Florida A. and M. College.

Even though she was not a member of the faculty of the high school at Pensacola, she volunteered her service to train the senior class in the presentation of their graduation speeches, which volunteer service was continued for the Lincoln High School graduating classes of 1925,1926, and 1927, the account of which is mentioned in the next chapter of this production.

The 1918-19 school term began with my appointment to the principalship of Public School 3, Pensacola, Florida, where I taught English, Mathematics, and science in the senior high school trades assisted by eight other teachers from grades five through ten. My appointment as principal followed the previous principal, Prof. L. A. Kirksey, who had served for several years.

Being a very young man, it was whispered that I was assuming quite a difficult task in accepting the responsibility as the principal of this school. I was principal for two years, after which I became the assistant principal the third year when the county school board upon the recommendation of the Trustee Board, decided to add $40.00 to the salary making the gross salary $720.00 and set the gross salary of the new principal at $1,000. It was not unusual for a segment of the parents and the Negro Supervisor to register complaints to the County Superintendent and the Board against the principal in the management of the school and thus brought influence to the Trustee Board in deciding on a new principal to supersede me as principal. Under my two-year tenure as principal and because of some improvements in the high school curriculum, instruction, organization and science equipment, the seniors who graduated were accepted in the freshman class not only at Florida A. and M. College but Fisk University, Nashville, Tennessee upon the submission of a transcript of their high school credits including the recommendation of the principal. Along with these requirements the applicants for admission to Fisk University were also to present physics notebooks showing that each applicant had performed in class with the approval of the principal the required number of experiments. Comments from some of the parents of the seniors whose children entered Fisk thought this was a significant advancement. With the new salary and the new principal in the 1920-21 school term, came the change in the name of the school from School #3 to Washington High School, Pensacola, Florida. The school had nine teachers including the principal and about 300 pupils. The grades in the school were from five through twelve. Six of the teachers taught pupils in grades five through eight.

The two years as principal of the high school afforded me with valuable teaching experience and insight into what one might expect in a position of leadership in education in a community, the perplexing situation in controls among pupils and cooperation from teachers in the school and the parents who were more directly concerned about the education of their children.

There is one memento that I have among the gifts in my possession which was presented to me at the high school graduation class night exercise by the seniors of that 1920 class, was a sterling silver shaving mug. The following are the names of the seniors on the card which accompanied the gift:

TO
Prof. A. QUINN JONES
COMPLIMENTS
OF
P. H. S. CLASS 1920

Mary Ellen Powerll
Janice Williams
J. Modest Thomas
Ruby James
Emma Hoffman
Janice DeVaughn
Viola Frear
Gladys Kelly

I cherish the memories and the small contribution that the recipient made toward the advancement and the beginning of their educational career.

REGISTRATION WITH BOARD

I was a Junior attending school at Florida A. and M. College when war began July 28, 1914 involving, twenty-nine nations. Many of the young men who were my schoolmates volunteered to enlist in the armed service of the United States. Some joined or enlisted in the army while others entered the U. S. Officers Training School, for the Government was in the process of increasing the number of men in the army. War was declared against Germany April 6, 1917. All men between the ages of 21 to 31 were required to register in preparation for conscription in the armed forces. I registered with my Draft Board a short time after my graduation from college. I was classified in class 1A since I had no dependents. There were tense moments after I received my classification which one was to carry with him wherever he went. Those with 1A classification were the first ones to be called for induction. Before I was called, however, I became married hence the Draft Board re-classified me and I was placed in class II. The sentiment at that time was that every man was to be a producer, preferably employed in production essential to the war effort. There was not any excuse for unemployment for the shipyards in Pensacola, Florida where I was teaching could use all the available man power in building steel ships for the government. After my school closed the April of 1918, I secured employment with the Pensacola Shipbuilding Co. at Warrington, Florida located on the Gulf of Mexico about fifteen miles from Pensacola. The electric trolley car lines were in use for transportation. Thousands of men worked at this plant performing varieties of labor in building these ships. Several ships were under construction at a time. I was a bolter for I did nothing else but that. Some men were riveters for they used powerful electric air hammers for doing this job. It was necessary that they be in good physical condition for this kind of work. Others were electricians, plumbers, carpenters, etc. Incidentally, the pay was much better than that of the teacher at that time. I worked on the job throughout the Summer until the opening of High School #3 in September 1918. On November the eleventh the Armistice was declared and the fighting ceased.

"OLD GAINESVILLE ALBUM"

Gainesville's Freemen's School

This handsome building, with Northern influence showing in its architecture, was the center of Negro education in Gainesville for many years. And when it was built, it was the center of much resentment in the town. It was called the Union Academy, and for many years functioned as a colored school at Northwest 1st Street at 7th Avenue — near today's Carver Branch Library. Records show the school was built by the United States Government shortly after the end of the Civil War, and was supported by contributions from Northern friends, the George Peabody Fund and the Board of Public Instruction. Even after Reconstruction, it received contributions from the North, and it is said teachers were better paid than those in white schools. The school's year was longer than in the white schools. At the time it was built, resentment about education for colored citizens was strong. Two early teachers, Harrie Barnes and Catherine Bent, wrote to a friend in 1866 that white boys sometimes threw "various kinds of missiles into our school room, in some cases aiming deliberately at the teacher and sometimes hitting them." In part, the resentment probably lingered from the Civil War, due to the use of textbooks in all schools which were heavily pro-Northern. Courses in the school were offered for levels from elementary through high school, and in 1880s, a normal department was added to train teachers for Florida schools. The building, originally designed for 120 students, had 175 when it opened, and in 1898 was crowded with more than 500 students, a condition in these days called overcrowding. Additions were made in 1898 which helped the school accommodate its students, but it was reported too small again in 1903. When Lincoln School was built in 1923, some of the crowding was eased. This vintage photograph is from the Florida State Museum collection.

UNION ACADEMY

CHAPTER III

EXPERIENCES TEACHING IN ALACHUA COUNTY

The incidents mentioned in the preceding CHAPTER leading to a change in the principal at Pensacola influenced me to accept the principalship of Union Academy, Gainesville, Florida, Alachua, County for the 1921-1922 winter school term of eight months at a salary of $1,000. It may be seen on my YEARS OF EXPERIENCE TEACHING CHART, that my tenure as a teacher in Alachua County and Gainesville, extended over a period of thirty-six years.

This is a copy of a letter to Dr. N. B. Young, President of Florida A. and M. College from Mr. Benj. F. Childs, a member of the Trustee Board of Union Academy seeking the recommendation of someone for the principalship of the school:

Gainesville, Florida, May 23, 1921

Mr. N. B. Young
Tallahassee, Fla.

Dear Sir:
Please put me in touch with a real Red-Blooded man for the principalship of Union Academy. No one knows better than you the type of man we are seeking.

The salary last year for the principal was $125.00 per month. We had fourteen teachers and an eight month's term.

There is also a chance to place his wife at a salary of from $50.00 to $75.00 per month.

Be careful to have all communications relative to the above addressed to me, as our trustees prefer to have first hand information in this matter.

Yours Very Truly,

Benj. F. Childs

The following is a reply to the above letter:

May 25, 1921

Mr. B. F. Childs
Gainesville, Florida

My Dear Mr. Childs:

I think Mr. Quinn Jones, Assistant Principal of the Pensacola High School, who once served as Principal of the same school, a good man for your Union Academy. He is a college graduate of this institution and has considerable experience in teaching and a man of excellent character. His wife, also is a teacher, or rather has had teaching experience. I am asking him to take up the matter with you if interesting to him.

In the meantime, I will be looking out for another man in the event Mr. Jones is not available. Hoping to be of service to you in the matter, and with kindest regards, I am

N. B. Young
President

On June 18, 1921, I filed a letter of application with the Alachua County Board of Public Instruction for the Principalship of Union Academy.

On July 8, 1921, a letter from the Trustees of Union Academy to the Alachua County School Board recommended me for appointment as principal. The letter of recommendation was signed by the following:

A. J. Parker
Benj. F. Childs
D. S. Rays
S. H. Hendley
E. Martin
G. W. Perkins

John W. Gass, Secretary
R. B. Ayer, Chairman

The Alachua County School Board in session on the above date (July 8) made the appointment.

Mrs. Jones, the two baby boys, and I arrived in Gainesville, August 30, 1921 on the T. and J. train. We were transferred from the Seaboard Air Line train at Lake City, Florida. The train station for the T. and J. was located at the intersection of West University Avenue and Sixth Street where the Trailway Bus Station is located. It was a rugged ride from Lake City to Gainesville. We made our abode at the home of Mrs. Debose, the mother of one of the pioneer teachers in the school, Mrs. Mamie E. Bryant. Later in the term, we were housed at the home of Mr. and Mrs. S. H. Hendley, Sr. where we lived for several terms, following that, we lived at the home of Mrs. Bellamy, Mother Mrs. Lucile DeBose, on Boundary Street (now N.W. Eighth Avenue) until November 1925 when we moved to the present location 1123 West Columbia Street (Now 1013 N.W. Seventh Avenue).

Entering upon my new assignment as the principal I found the community under the leadership of the Trustees of the school involved in an organized effort to raise $1,600 to insure that the school term might be eight months for the Alachua County Board had only appropriated sufficient county tax monies to pay the teachers for six months. The city was divided into districts and solicitors covered the districts weekly and made weekly financial reports on collections at the school each Sunday afternoon during the school term. The teachers sold sandwiches during lunch hour at school along with concerts, plays, fish fries, etc. to augment the collections. The effort was spearheaded by members of the Trustee Board of the School, viz:

Dr. R. B. Ayer, Chairman
Mr. D. S. Rays
Mr. Benj. F. Childs
Mr. G. W. Perkins
Mr. E. Martin
Mr. John W. Gass

Mr. A. J. Parker
M. S. H. Hendley, Jr.

The combined effort of the patrons and citizens insured sufficient funds, $1,600, for the school to operate for the full term of eight months.

The teachers were as follows:

A. Quinn Jones, Principal, 10th Grade Subjects
D. E. White, Assistant Prin., 9th Grade Subjects
Mrs. Amy Davis, 8th Grade
Miss Lucille Brown, 7th Grade
Miss Ella Childs, 6th Grade
Mrs. Mamie E. Perkins, 5th Grade
Mrs. Hallie Q. Madison, 4th Grade
Mrs. Ida Williams, 3rd Grade
Miss Malissa Hendley, 3rd Grade
Mrs. Mamie E. Bryan, 2nd Grade
Mrs. Adrianna Ayer
Mrs. Judith P. Rainey, 1st Grade
Mrs. Bessie M. Brown, Primer

My previous church home and membership at Allen Chapel A. M. E. Church, Pensacola was transferred to Bethel A. M. E. Church across the street from the school under the pastorate of Rev. J. N. Young. Several years later in 1932, the church was re-located at 600 N. W. Seventh Avenue – Greater Bethel A. M. E. Church.

Gainesville like most towns lacked automobiles as a means for transportation when I arrived here. There were a few Negro taxi drivers with automobiles who followed this kind of business. One had to do much walking. Automobiles were too expensive for the average person to own one.

Having been assigned to teach Summer school in 1923 at Arredonda, Fla., seven miles West of Gainesville, involved the need for some kind of transportation. I went to my school on the early Seaboard Air Line passenger train that left Gainesville via old

Arredonda for Cedar Keys and returned late in the afternoon stopping at Arredonda on the return trip to Gainesville and on to Waldo, Fla. This schedule was very inconvenient, therefore, I went to the bicycle shop the same afternoon, purchased a used bicycle, and I was on my way to school the next morning and returned on schedule time every day during the three-month school term. There was a hard surfaced road the entire distance except from the railroad station off the highway for a short distance. At a normal rate of speed, it required 35 or 40 minutes to make the trip.

The bicycle as a means for transportation became a necessity for my use around town in the city. This cycle was my vehicle for the four Summers following the first Summer of teaching at Arredonda.

Following the last Summer of teaching there, I began buying a small Studebacker car for transportation purposes. However, I continued to use my bicycle for an extended time thereafter.

Mrs. J. P. Rainey and Mrs. Bessie M. Brown assisted me as teachers at this school during my five Summers of service. They did an excellent job for many of the pupils continued their winter schooling by going to the Gainesville Lincoln Public School.

ATHLETICS – 1921 TO 1957

In order to promote athletics in the school at the beginning of my service as principal, Mr. Charles S. Chestnut, Sr. volunteered his service from his personal business as mortician with my approval worked with the boys and girls in athletics coaching the football team and basketball for boys and girls. This was done as a public service to the school. He gave quite an abundance of his time in the afternoons coaching the teams. It was because of his interest and enthusiasm in athletics that by the end of the third football season in 1923, Lincoln High School ended the season as the champion high school team in the state. The players on this team were:

> James Roberts
> Andrew Philips
> Clifton Aiken
> Edgar Daniels, Jr.
> Willie Stephens
> James Mathews
> Eric Roberts
> Joseph Dennis
> Benjamin Hill
> James Ingrim
> Waymon Haile
> Alphonso Lewis
> Johnnie Glasper
> Alex C. Duval
> Walter Daniels

MASCOTS:

> Charles Chestnut, Jr.
> Bubber Robinson

A. Quinn Jones, Principal and A. O. Jenkins, assistant principal were the only men members on the faculty to give assistance to Mr. Chestnut whose service will long be remembered.

A. Quinn Jones, Sr.

1013 N. W. SEVENTH AVENUE
Gainesville, Florida   32601
June 14, 1975.

Mr. Charles S. Chestnut, Sr.
Chestnut's Funeral Home
Gainesville, Florida   32601

Dear Mr. Chestnut:

Alachua County is in the process of celebrating the
Bi-Centennial which terminates July 4, 1976. Activities
are in progress in Gainesville and cities throughout Florida
commemorating this great event. You and many of our older
citizens have been a part of the history-making events among
Black people in Florida and this community.

I am aware of the fact that Hughes and Chestnut Funeral
Establishment was a pioneer among Black Undertaking Business-
es in Florida. Your business has operated over fifty years
and at the present time is among the top establishments in
the state of Florida. It was through your untiring efforts
over so many years that has made this business what it is
today, and is being ably carried on by your descendants. There
are also other branches of Chestnut's Funeral Establishments.

I pause here and note that your interests in the community consumed a great amount of your time taken from your
business. You volunteered your service to coach football and
basketball teams without compensation during the early years
of Lincoln High School. The County School Board did not provide funds to hire an athletic coach. It was in 1923 that
you developed the first Lincoln football team and attained
champions among the high school teams of Florida.

Furthermore, several morticians received their intern-
training at Chestnut's Funeral Home under your supervision.

In 1940, you were President of the Local Chapter of the
Florida State Negro Business League.

You served as YMCA secretary during World War I.

You served as a member of the Lincoln High School Advisory Board.

So many years, you rendered dedicated service to humanity.

I extend to you commendations and hearty felicitations
on this occasion.

Sincerely Yours,

A. Quinn Jones
Retired Principal

42

Mr. Joseph J. Dennis, a member of the first graduating class of eight members, a graduate of Clark College, Atlanta, returned to Lincoln as a teacher of History and Mathematics and assumed the duties of football coach during the 1929 season. This was the beginning of a regular member of the school staff to be given the coaching responsibility. After serving on Lincoln High school faculty for one or two years, he was called back to Clark College to teach in the mathematics department. He continued his education at Northwestern University where he earned the Ph. D. degree in Mathematics and for many years has been head of the department of mathematics at Clark and professor of mathematics.

Mr. Simeon Williams and Mr. Gaston T. Cook assisted in athletic coaching two or three years intervening.

Mr. Thomas B. Mcpherson, a recent graduate of Florida A. and M. College, also a graduate of Lincoln High School, joined the faculty of Lincoln High School as teacher of history and was assigned the duties of football and basketball coach for the 1932 season. He has done an excellent job in this area over the years as coach, teacher of physical education, athletic director or head of the physical education department as well as city wide recreation director.

Lincoln High School has produced several State Championship football teams and a National High school team under his guidance. He has been a faculty member of this school for thirty-five years.

Several of the teachers working in his department were once his students or members of the teams he coached. He has the B. S. degree from Florida A. and M. College and Xavier University, New Orleans; acquired the M.A. degree in Physical Education from Columbia University, N.Y.

Lincoln High School was preceded by a much earlier school known as Union Academy located on the grounds of the present recreation center. It was organized in 1866 under the auspices of the

Freedmen's Bureau, afterwards came under the control of the Alachua County School Board.

In 1897, two year of junior high school above the eighth grade elementary school was offered as a part of the curriculum of this institution.

In 1923, the school moved to a new site when the name changed to Lincoln and in 1925 became a four-year senior high school.

During these early years, the school did not have a full time music teacher, nevertheless, music activities were emphasized throughout the school. The school took advantage of the music abilities of faculty members on the teaching staff and assigned music instruction along with their regular classroom teaching duties, and therefore, directed the choral class and related music activities.

The following are some of the teachers who were chief musicians who directed the Choral Class and other related activities:

> Mrs. Judith P. Rainey, Primary Grade Teacher
> Mrs. Mayme T. Cook, High School Teacher
> Mrs. Daphne A. Duval, High School Teacher
> Mrs. Frederica M. Jones, High School Teacher

Since the year 1951, these teachers were appointed full time music teachers on Lincoln faculty:

> 1946-47 - Miss Lorraine D. Hawkins
> 1947-48 - Miss Naomi Britton

Mrs. Wilhelmina W. Johnson and Mrs. Geraldine Y. Miller and Mr. Jerry C. Miller, Director of Lincoln School Band and Head of the Music Department.

The department of music at this institution including the choral class and the band has made an excellent contribution to the

44

cultural advancement and appreciation of music and fine arts among the students as well as the community.

TEACHERS AND EXTRA-CLASS DUTIES

A teacher well prepared in piano and other skills in music has always been an asset to any school faculty. It was not until the school term 1946-47 that the schools of the county and the state provided for special music teachers to conduct all the music activities or instruction in the elementary and high school departments.

When I assumed the duties of principal, Mrs. Judith P. Rainey and Mrs. Bessie M. Brown, Primary teachers, did all of the playing and directing for the daily school devotionals exercises, school programs of various kinds, and school closing programs. Their services in this capacity extended over a period of several years.

The Music Committee was one of Lincoln High School's important ones since it was responsible for the music activities throughout the school. Mrs. Lucille White, a teacher of English and Latin, and Mrs. Agnes M. Jones, eighth grade teacher, became members of this committee.

Mrs. Thelma Gaines who was well trained in piano served on the music committee and did much of the playing for various school activities.

Mrs. Frederica M. Williams became a member of the committee when she joined the school staff in 1929. Miss Daphne Alexander and Mrs. Mayme T. Cook were appointed teachers on the Lincoln High school faculty and served on the same committee. The principal relied on these individuals to be responsible for the music activities throughout the school.

During different periods of time over the years, both Frederica M. Jones and Mrs. Daphne Alexander-Duval served as head teachers of the Elementary Department of Lincoln. They directed the musical parts of elementary as well as high school assemblies and special programs; trained children in connection with preparation for musical activities; rehearsed pupils and accompanied elementary school closing exercises in music and high school commencement exercises.

Again, it has been stated on previous pages in this document relative to the various capacities in which Mrs. Frederica M. Jones has served Lincoln in connection with other duties of directing the music until the year 1946-47 when a full-time music teacher was provided for the school, she headed the High School English Department for more than twelve years--until her retirement in 1966.

By attending Summer school and taking Extension in service courses, she was awarded both the B.S. and M.S. degrees from Florida A. and M. University.

ADMINISTRATIVE ASSISTANTS

Immediately following her graduation from Lincoln High School in the year 1926, Mrs. Thelma M. Williams-Jordan began her career as teacher in the public schools of Alachua County. She taught in several schools and through in-service training, taking extension courses in winter along with Summer school attendance was awarded the B. S. degree followed by continued Summer school attendance, was awarded the M. A. degree from New York University. She came to Lincoln and was given the responsibility of Head Teacher of the Elementary Department. In the year 1943-44. She rendered effective service in this capacity continuously to the 1956 school term when the Alachua County Board of Public Instruction appointed her principal of the A. Quinn Jones Elementary School (formerly Lincoln Elementary Department) when the high school moved to the new facility. She has been principal for twelve years. The school has an enrollment of approximately 800 pupils and twenty-seven teachers.

It has been mentioned on previous pages of Mrs. Daphne Alexander-Duval having been a high school teacher of mathematics, and teacher-training courses. In the year 1946-47, she was appointed to assist the principal as coordinator along with some counseling duties in the high school, all of which were previously performed by the principal. She performed in this capacity to the year 1956 when the school moved to the new Lincoln school plant, she became coordinator of Instruction and Dean of Girls. She has in more recent years become an assistant principal of Lincoln High School. She holds both the B.S. and M. Ed. degrees from Florida A. and M. University.

A CHALLENGE

The school and community were jubilant over the designation of Lincoln by the State Department of Education as one of the first two Negro high schools becoming [an] accredited four-year senior high school in Florida in 1926. I recall it was a rainy day before the holiday season in 1925 that Dr. R. M. Sealey, State Inspector of High Schools, made an official visit for the purpose of making an inspection and study of the operation of the school to determine whether it met accreditization standards. It has met standards every year since that date, even though at times, difficulties arose in staffing the school with properly certificated and otherwise qualified teachers.

It occurs to me momentarily that Lincoln encountered grave obstacles which were surmounted in the year 1925 when it became a four-year high school and graduated the first high school class. The teachers, high school students, parents, and senior class, worked throughout the term from its beginning, by sponsoring projects to raise money for the library to buy books in sufficient numbers to meet standards. Book showers were held.

A science fee of $5.00 was paid by each member of the senior class along with financial efforts from other various sources enabled the school to buy science equipment that the senior class in physics in particular might be able to perform the necessary number of experiments to meet standards in this subject and to permit experimentation for the class in general science and biology. The principal taught the physics class and headed the science department.

It was shocking to everybody when the Alachua County Board of Public Instruction annoinced a shortage of funds for operating the schools and ordered the Superintendent E. R. Simmons to close Lincoln at the end of the sixth month. However, this was a challenge to the Lincoln School and the community not to let this tragedy befall us. The Advisory Board of Lincoln High School, the teachers, the Parent-Teachers Association, and the community accepted the challenge and pledged to give their full support by subscribing the needed amount of money to pay the teachers in full for the extra two months to maintain the full eight-month school term. The financial goal was achieved by payment of subscriptions from parents, patrons, and friends of the school and also from monies received through school programs, selling on the school grounds, solicitation from churches and other community organizations. The financial drive was overwhelmingly successful. As a result, this enabled the first and only senior class of eight students to graduate from Gainesville's first senior high school for Negroes. This is possibly one of the outstanding achievements of my years teaching.

THE COMMENCEMENT PROGRAM FOLLOWS:

COMMENCEMENT

LINCOLN HIGH SCHOOL
Monday Evening May 18th, 1925
8:00 P.M.

Mt. Pleasant Methodist Church

* * * * * * * * * *

- CLASS ROLL -
Joseph Oliver Acosta
Benjamin Franklin Childs, Jr.

Edgar Rudolph Daniels, Jr.
Joseph James Dennis
Carlos Earl Haile
Emmette Alveo Londy

Eric Biltmore Roberts

Claronell Gloria Smith

- CLASS OFFICERS -
Joseph James Dennis, President
Edgar Rudolph Daniels, Vice President
Emmette Alveo Londy, Secretary
Carlos Earle Haile, Treasurer
* * * * *
CLASS FLOWER – Pink Carnation
CLASS COLORS – Gray and Pink
MOTTO: "Rowing Not Drifting"

- CLASS NIGHT EXERCISES -
Friday, May 15, 8:00 P.M.

Chorus
Invocation
President's Address .... Joseph James Dennis
Instrumental Solo.. Julius O. Acosta
Class History.. Eric B. Roberts
Instrumental Solo.. Claronell G. Smith
Class Poem.. Emmette A. Londy
Jubilee, "Swing Low, Sweet Chariot" .... Senior Class
Class Will.. Edgar R. Daniels
Vocal Solo .... Benjamin F. Childs,

49

A. Quinn Jones, Sr.

	Jr.
Oar Oration	Julius O. Acosta
Response	John F. Jones, Pres. of Junior Class
Vocal Duet	Misses Smith and Londy
Class Prophecy ...	Carlos E. Haile

Class Song
Benediction

ANNUAL SERMON
Sunday May 17, 3:00 P. M.

Preclude
Processional
Coronation
Scription Lesson
Invocation
Anthem, "Arise and Praise Ye the Lord", (Hiram Simmons)……..……………..Choral Class
Annual Sermon……………………………Rev. H. M. Collins, D. D.
Pastor of Bethel A. M. Church
Anthem, "The Lord Is My Light", (Hiram Simmons)………………….…….Choral Class
Offertory
Music (a)   Instrumental Solo
(b)   Jubilee
Benediction
Recessional

* * * * * * * * * *

GRADUATING EXERCISE
Monday May 18, 8:00 P. M.

Processional
Chorus, "Lift Every Voice and Sing", (Rosmond Johnson and James W. Johnson) – Choral
Class
Invocation
Chorus, "To Thee, O Country", (Lane and Eichberg)…………………….Choral Class
Oration, "The Patriotism Of the American Negro"………………….Edgar R. Daniels, Jr.

51

A. Quinn Jones, Sr.

Oration, "The Test of Greatness"...Carlos E. Haile

Jubilee

Oration, "The Negro's Contribution to Literature"............................Claronell G. Smith

Oration, "Self Help"...Benjamin F. Childs

Address,..
....Dr. J. R. E. Lee,
President
Fla. A. and M.
College

Presentation of Diplomas

Prize Awards

Chorus, "O, Hail, Day of Rest" (Mrs. Adaline H. Beery)....................Choral Class

Benediction

DIFFICULT FINDING PREPARED TEACHERS

Some times over the early years, it was difficult to employ satisfactory prepared or qualified teachers to meet the needs of the school. Lack of competitive salaries and a shortage in the supply of trained teachers graduating from higher institutions. Earlier, the principal recruited the teachers mainly from those trained at Florida A. and M. College. After students began graduating from Lincoln High School in 1925, the principal began to advise students furthering their education in various colleges to do their major studies in college areas where demands were greatest for employment in education. Four years following the first high school graduates, the principal began recommending the hiring of some of the recent graduates to fill positions on the Lincoln Faculty. For several years, college graduates who completed high school graduation from Lincoln were employed to teach in various grades of the elementary as well as the high school. Moreover, Graduates of Lincoln High School could be found teaching in schools throughout the city and the county. As the years passed, teachers' salaries became more attractive and consequently, teaching positions became easier to fill. The beginning salary for the Negro teacher in 1921 was $40.00.

DEATH OF PRINCIPAL'S WIFE

February 15, 1928 culminated in death the life activities of Mrs. Agnes M. Jones, the wife of the principal who was a member of the Lincoln High School faculty, a dedicated and ardent school teacher for a number of years, a religious worker, a member of Bethel A. M. E. Church, active and interested in young people's activities, a religious, a staunch Christian and a devoted wife. She left four children: A. Quinn, Jr., Oliver Hugh, Lydia Alveda, and Vera Hortense. A. Quinn, Jr. died February 13, 1996.

Mr. J. Franklin Jones, Jr., a graduate of the second Lincoln High School class and a student of Clark College, Atlanta, completed school term and the class work left by the death of the Principal's wife.

After graduating from Clark College in 1932 with the B.S. degree, he again became a member of the Lincoln faculty instructing students in science. He was head of the science department for several years. While in service as teacher, he continued his education attending Summer school, and was awarded the M.A. degree from Atlanta University. He has served on the faculty for more than thirty years.

Several years later, Quinn, Jr., and Oliver graduated from Lincoln High School and Florida A. and M. College with bachelor degrees. Daughters, Lydia and Vera, attended upper elementary and high school at Davis Street Elementary School and Stanton High School Jacksonville, Fla. Lydia graduated from Stanton High School and Florida A. and M. College with the B.A. degree. Vera, graduated from Lincoln High School, Gainesville, and Florida Memorial College, St. Augustine, attaining the B.S. degree. Previously, she received a diploma in cosmetology.

The two boys were born in Pensacola, Florida. Although we were living in Gainesville, Lydia was also born in Pensacola and Vera was born in Gainesville, Florida.

Referring to the previous paragraph on the training or education of the children, it might be mentioned that Quinn, Jr., was awarded the M.A. degree from Atlanta University and has practically completed requirements for the Ed. D. degree from Pennsylvania State University. He was employed as principal of Lanier Junior High School, Ft. Lauderdale, Florida. Later, he was awarded the Ed. D. degree, Nova University. Oliver was awarded the M. Ed. degree by Tuskegee Institute and has done a great amount of graduate work at Indiana University. He was principal of the A. L. Mebane High School, Alachua, County. Later, he was awarded the Ed. D. degree, Nova University. Lydia was awarded the M. Ed. degree by Tuskegee Institute and has done additional graduate work at Northwestern and Temple Universities. She was employed as one of the instructors in the Department of English at Central Florida Junior College, Ocala, Florida. Vera has acquired additional courses at Jacksonville

University. She is employed as a teacher at the Bethune Elementary School, Jacksonville, Florida.

I was joined in wedlock to Mrs. Frederica M. Williams, December 19, 1937. She was a teacher in the school for eight years before this date. She had been a quality teacher in the Duval County School System before her appointment to the Lincoln School. She died October 14, 1994.

EXPERIENCE TEACHING IN ALACHUA COUNTY

The 1929-30 school term was another year that was very arduous for teachers, parents, and students. The county school funds for operating schools for a full term were not sufficient, hence tuition fees were required of all the children to raise funds to operate school for two months to maintain the regular eight-month school term. Money was collected weekly by the teachers. The following is a sample of a week's Bulletin Board Poster or Booster Report displayed on the Board in the principal's office during the campaign:

Lincoln High School
Information For Teachers

1. Let our slogan be an aggregate collection of $100 a week.
2. Get out among the parents so that the collection of these fees might amount to an aggregate of $100 next week.
3. The collection for the first week was $37.85.
4. Miss Adger led the faculty this past week in collecting more than ten dollars.

Week Ending October 12, 1929

Mr. Dennis and Mrs. Days led faculty in collecting tuition. They collected more than five dollars each. Aggregate collection a little less than last week.

* * * * * *

The collection of tuition fees for the past week ending October 25th was low, amounting to about $20. Let all the teachers re-double their efforts during this week and continue. We must collect $1,000 dollars by Christmas. Mrs. Days led in collections last week.

* * * * * *

November 6, 1929

Miss Alexander led faculty in collecting $18.00 last week in tuition fees. About forty dollars collected.

BEAUTIFYING SCHOOL GROUNDS

A Lincoln High School Advisory Board composed of five patrons replaced the old Union Academy Trustee Board of eight members when the school moved to the school site at West Columbia Street (now N. W. Seventh Avenue). The first effort to beautify the grounds was made through the Advisory Board by planting three or four oak trees about ten feet tall on the East and South sides of the building. All the trees died except the one on the East which survived and grew into a massive oak which stood for forty-four years before being destroyed by the city in making way for paving the street East of the building in 1967.

About six years passed before a gigantic effort was made by the teachers and pupils with the cooperation of the patrons to begin foundation planting around the base of the building.

Plots were designated and assigned to each teacher and her grade to be responsible for beautifying with shrubbery, nursing it until each gained a foothold. There was never a more enthusiastic group of people working toward a common goal. Most of the shrubbery was donated by solicitations. Sidewalks around the building were constructed through the cooperation of the city of Gainesville by city prisoners. The materials discarded from the renovation of the Seagle Building and other sources were donated for the job. It was through the efforts of Mr. Charles S. Chestnut, Sr. and the Advisory Board that this project came about. Now, more than thirty years afterward, these walks are still in use.

In 1942, National Youth Administration work students in the high school department under the supervision of Mr. Thornton Roberts, D. C. T. Instructor, constructed the walk from the South East corner of the school building to the street. The athletic department supplied materials for building a concrete play court on the South side of the school auditorium. These were monuments to all those teachers, Mr. T. B. McPherson, and pupils along with Mr. Thornton W. Roberts, who participated in making these conveniences possible by their efficient supervision. It seems a bit interesting to writer when he recalls having lent helping hands along with interested teachers and coaches of athletic teams in basketball to build courts back of the building to the West for games, and later a court at the North entrance to the building, enclosed first with sack cloths and later with pine slabs with over-head lights for playing night games. Spectators at times standing in the cold weather were not deterred nor were the participating teams for the general interest overshadowed the disadvantages. These were the play facilities until 1956, when the new Lincoln High School was occupied.

ADDITIONS TO BUILDING

The auditorium to the building with a seating capacity of 825 was constructed at a cost of approximately $27,000 and the auditorium chairs were installed in time for the 1928 Commencement Exercises.

The seven all contained Class-Room Annex for elementary pupils was constructed about 1950 but nevertheless double school sessions were still necessary intermittently until 1956-57.

The cafeteria was constructed and occupied in 1955.

A STORY OF LIBRARY SHELVES FOR THE LIBRARY ROOM
AND TABLES FOR THE SCIENCE ROOM FOLLOWS:

When school opened in August 1923, the regular toilets in the building could not be used because there were no sanitary sewer lines in this area of Gainesville. Therefore out-door toilet facilities were built for the boys and another for the girls. They were built with a very good grade of lumber. They were in use by the students for about a month, while the city was extending the sewer from University Avenue, a distance of seven blocks -- to the school and the necessary connections made. After connections were made to the city sewer line, the materials which were used to construct the toilets were salvaged but were not discarded for there were other needs for it. The room designated for the school library was minus of any library equipment, no shelves, tables, chairs, nor other necessities. Hence the principal with some of the eleventh grade boys used this salvaged lumber from the wood out-door toilets and made several stacks of library shelves and beautified them with golden oak varnish.

Throughout this school term and the next term when the school attained a four-year senior high school status, efforts continued. The principal with the help of the eleventh and twelfth grade boys and other miscellaneous help from the teachers and the children, by the end of this school year, one library table was made, another library table along with four or more chairs were purchased; a large table was made for the science room, sufficient for mounting experiment equipment in general science, biology, and physics. The principal taught physics, solid geometry, Latin and trigonometry classes. The library was under the supervision of the English teacher, Miss Eloise Perkins. Webster's International Dictionary was among the first new books purchased for the library.

Mrs. M. F. Days, a teacher and president of the Excelsior Reading Club, presented the library with several volumes of literature by Negro Authors and Writers; viz: Dunbar, James Weldon Johnson, Booker T. Washington, etc.

During these years, the school and community had to rely on self-help in order to supply the children with some of the most badly needed materials. The County School Board through the Trustees appropriated $125 which enabled the principal to purchase a compound microscope, and certain other standard equipment for teaching general science, biology and physics. Science fees were assessed the students taking science to increase the supply of equipment over the years. More than a decade had passed before the science room was equipped with gas and a sink with running water to permit the teaching of chemistry.

THE PRINCIPAL AND CONTINUOUS STUDY

Even though I had acquired the bachelor's degree, I felt that the changes taking place in education in Florida and the South, generally required one to continue to improve one's self while in the teaching service if one expected to make it a career. My salary as may be seen in the chart was very meager for Negro teachers and principals received salaries from 20 to 25 percent lower than that of white teaching personnel with the same qualifications. In considering schools where I might matriculate for advanced study for several weeks during the Summer, I discovered that Hampton Institute, Virginia, was the only Negro institution in the South that offered graduate courses leading to the M.A. degree in the field of education and related areas. The Summer of 1930, when I entered Hampton Summer School to begin work toward an advanced degree, Negroes were not accepted for study in Southern White colleges and universities. I could not attend the University of Florida located about six or seven blocks from my residence. Therefore, the Summers, 1930, 1931, 1933, and 1934 attendance at Hampton permitted me to complete class attendance, courses, and academic requirements and during the school term I completed the writing of master's degree thesis which enabled me to meet all requirements and the M.A. degree in Education and Social Studies was awarded at the regular commencement of 1935.

Ironically, as it might seem, I could not use the University of Florida Library nor withdraw books which I needed for research in writing thesis. I cannot forget the generosity of Dr. A. R. Meade who withdrew books from the library for my use and also the late Dr. Alfred Crage who gave helpful suggestions when I was in the process of writing. Both of these fine gentlemen were faculty members of the University College of Education. The secretary of Dean Tolbert, Dean of Students, typed the three copies of my thesis that were required for presentation to the Hampton Institute Graduate Committee.

The Summer 1936, following graduation from Hampton, I matriculated in the College of Education, New York University where I was admitted to a planned program of study with emphasis in Secondary Education leading to the Ph. D. degree. I attended the Summer of 1937 also. The war in progress at this time interrupted and I returned to N.Y.U. the 1952 Summer Session. The intervening Summer of 1944, principals in Negro schools of the state of Fla. were given aid to attend a Graduate Workshop at Florida A. and M. College. In 1948, a preplanning workshop for teachers preceded the opening of Alachua County Schools. More than half the required program planned was completed. The Minimum Foundation Program of Florida Education adopted in 1946-1947 required school principals to be on duty for twelve months which interrupted further pursuit of my planned Program of educational improvement at N.Y.U. I submitted my planned course of studies, with the approval of the Dean of Education and filed the outline of courses with the Florida State Department of Education with the view of qualifying for the Rank I Florida Teacher's Certificate.

Commencement Exercises

of

Hampton Institute

OGDEN HALL

Tuesday afternoon, May 29, 1934, at 2:15 o'clock

Program

Organ Prelude

Invocation   REV. S. ARTHUR DEVAN

They Look Like Men of War

1. Hark! listen to the trumpeters,
   They call for volunteers,
   On Zion's bright and flow'ry mount,
   Behold the officers.

2. Their horses white, their armor
     bright,
   With courage bold they stand,
   Enlisting soldiers for their King,
   To march to Canaan's land.

3. It sets my heart quite in a flame,
   A soldier thus to be,
   I will enlist, gird on my arms,
   And fight for liberty.

4. We want no cowards in our band
   That will their colors fly;
   We call for valiant-hearted men,
   Who're not afraid to die.

Refrain:
They look like men, they look like men,
They look like men of war;
All armed and dressed in uniform,
They look like men of war,

AUDIENCE

Address   MRS. MARY McLEOD BETHUNE
                                           President of Bethune-Cookman College

We Are Climbing Jacob's Ladder

AUDIENCE (standing)

Presentation of Prizes and Awards

Albert Howe Prize in Agriculture
Calliope Literary Society Prizes
The James E. Gregg Prizes
The George Foster Peabody Prize
The Lilla M. Mitchell Special Prize in Home Economics
Scholarship Awards by the Young Men's Christian Associ-
     ation of Hampton Institute

Announcement of Honorary Scholarships

Conferring of Diplomas and Degrees

PRESIDENT ARTHUR HOWE

Alma Mater Song (Words are printed on the last page.)

The audience will please stand both as the procession enters
and as it leaves the hall.

61

ORDER OF THE ACADEMIC PROCESSION

Marshall

President and Speaker of the Day

Chaplain, Trustees, Directors of the Schools

Administrative and Educational Boards

Assistant Marshalls

College Faculty

Phenix School Faculty

Trade School Faculty

Alumni

and the following

(by degree and diploma groups according to height)

CANDIDATES for DEGREES and DIPLOMAS

THE COLLEGE

Candidates for Degree of MASTER OF ARTS

Clarence Wilbert Galloway   Petersburg, Va.
    B. S. Wilberforce University, 1922
Elmer Theodore Hawkins   Chestertown, Md.
    A. B. Morgan College, 1926

Candidates for Degree of BACHELOR OF SCIENCE

Degree with Distinction

Gertrude Irene Ball	Luella Hawkins
Isabella Strange Fletcher	Anne Eliza McKay
Luther Hilton Foster, Jr.	Lawson Sessions Randall
Hilda Banks Hall	Louis Shulterbrandt

School of Agriculture

Thomas Frederick Carter ....Coke, Va.
Robert Thomas Church ....Athens, Ga.
Manuel Huston Crockett ....Mascot, Tenn.
Benjamin Franklin Garrett ....Guthrie, Okla.
Iro Sylvester Glover ....Aiken, S. C.
William Henry Holtzclaw, Jr. ....Utica Institute, Miss.
Lawson Sessions Randall ....Hampton Institute, Va.
Isaac Cephus Rogers ....Zebulon, N. C.
Philip Tebee Seabrook ....Frogmore, S. C.
Walter Leo Webb ....Dermott, Ark.
Norman Payne Wilson ....Texarkana, Ark.
Merritt Milford Woodson ....Lynchburg, Va.

School of Business

Helen Eugenia Arrant ....Pine Bluff, Ark.
Gertrude Irene Ball ....Minor, Va.
William Harney Clifton Bradford ....Louisville, Ky.
Fred Benjamin Brooks ....Mounds, Okla.
Ella Louise Brown ....Hampton, Va.
Luther Hilton Foster, Jr. ....Petersburg, Va.
Pearl Corrine Gray ....Baltimore, Md.
William Settles Hardin ....Bardstown, Ky.
Sara Elizabeth Harris ....Newport News, Va.
Audrey Mae Cecelia Hill ....Baltimore, Md.
William Pate Inman ....Knoxville, Tenn.

Pearl Wilma Long ....W. Ashville, N. C.
Regina Joan Monroe ....Tulsa, Okla.
Isadore Boyd Oglesby ....Durham, N. C.
Ella Louise Phillips ....Brunswick, Ga.
Martha Annie Ann Elizabeth Riddick ....Hampton, Va
Thelma Mary Rippy ....Brookfield Center, Conn.
John Herman Henry Sengstacke ....Savannah, Ga.
Louis Shulterbrandt ....St. Thomas, V. I.
Mary Elizabeth Tonkins ....Hampton, Va.

School of Education

*Lillian Adelaide Carter ....Phoebus, Va.
*Thelma Louise Duncan ....Hampton, Va.
Harry Lee Faggett ....Greensboro, N. C.
Hilda Banks Hall ....Louisville, Ky.
Clarence Portfield Harris ....Wilmington, Del.
Homer Leroy Hines ....Newport News, Va.
Regina Letitia Jackson ....Norfolk, Va.
*Grace Viola Stewart Jenkins ....Newport News, Va.
Major Boyd Jones ....Gum Fork, Va.
Calvin George Lambson ....Baltimore, Md.
Melvin Edward Lancaster ....Washington, D. C.
William Jay Laws ....Seaford, Del.
Eliza Jessie Mae Lemon ....Columbia, S. C.
Austin Alexander Lewis ....Mathews, Va.
Emma Lewis ....Winston-Salem, N. C.
Stephen Nathaniel Lewis ....Jacksonville, Fla.
*Marie McIver ....Weldon, N. C.
Anne Eliza McKay ....Fayetteville, N. C.
Beth Constance Mitchell ....Gatesville, N. C.
Mary Cordelia Moore ....Detroit, Mich.
Evelyn Levater Paige ....Grafton, Va.
Mary Lynn Saunders ....Selden, Va.
Nannie Pearl Scales ....Roanoke, Va.
Florence Stevens Smith ....Wilkes Barre, Pa.
Rheba Georgetta Smith ....New York, N. Y.
Helen Maxine Stephens ....Tampa, Fla.
Clorean Acelnor Terrell ....Henderson, N. C.
Lacy Louise Truehart ....Hampton, Va.
Allen Easter Weatherford ....Charlottesville, Va.
*Florence Jamison Webb ....Dermott, Ark.
*Lillie Alice Motley Wilson ....Snow Hill, Ala.
Stephen Junius Wright ....Brooklyn, N. Y.
Sylvester Yates ....Philadelphia, Pa.

School of Home Economics

Minta Hanks Davis ....Washington, D. C.
Glandora Ione Duggins ....Jamesville, N. C.
Murlenun Bowman Hibbler ....Jackson, Miss.
Georgia Muriël Little ....Mobile, Ala.
Alberta Elaine Mebane ....Alachua, Fla.
Luvenia Cecil Miller ....Leaksville, N. C.
Urath Rosetta Peters ....Baltimore, Md.
Thelma Cleo Powell ....Tulsa, Okla.
Ella May Puryear ....Baltimore, Md.
Zxlema Patton Smith ....Alcorn, Miss.
Irene Palmer Stitt ....Brooklyn, N. Y.
Camille Sophronia Washington ....Baton Rogue, La.
Rosa Virginia Wilhoite ....Newport, R. I.
Elouise Williams ....Norfolk, Va.
Brenda Hazel Yancey ....Atlanta, Ga.
Charity A. T. Zomelo ....Keta, Gold Coast, W. A.

Library School

Frances Elizabeth Brown ....Cleveland, O.
    A. B. Cleveland, Western Reserve University, 1932
Ida Mae Buckley ....Enterprise, Miss.
    A. B. Tougaloo College, 1933
Maisie Viola Curtis ....Phoebus, Va.
James Everett Coby ....Marshall, Tex.
    A. B. Bishop College, 1932
Luella Hawkins ....Dayton, O.
    B. S. Wilberforce University, 1933
Maud Rebecca Hill ....Ft. Smith, Ark.
Ann LaPerle Howard ....Hampton, Va.
Wallace Van Jackson ....Richmond, Va.
Mayme Garland Marguerite Lovell ....Atlanta, Ga.
    A. B. Wiley College, 1929
Annie Charliese Pendarvis ....Orangeburg, S. C.
    A. B. Claflin College, 1930
Margaret Elizabeth Pendergrass ....Springfield, Ill.
Rose Elizabeth Sully ....Richmond, Va.
    A. B. Virginia Union University, 1933
Selena Lucille Warren ....Durham, N. C.
    A. B. Howard University, 1932
Sara Jane Watts ....Atlanta, Ga.
    A. B. Spelman College, 1933

School of Music

*Reuben Tolakele Caluza ....Edendale, Natal, S. A.
Joel Tyler Carter ....Camden, N. J.
Marjorie Geraldine Dandy ....Greenwood, S. C.
Isabella Strange Fletcher ....Connellsville, Pa.
Edmonia Lucile Johnson ....Anderson, S. C.
Ida May Northern ....New York, N. Y.
Solomon Phillips, Jr. ....Hampton, Va.
Spencer Jordan Satchell, Jr. ....Hampton, Va.

Trade School
Building Construction

*Robert Joshua Blanton ....Denmark, S. C.
Nathaniel Nelson ....Kansas City, Mo.
David Eugene Smith ....Staunton, Va.
Carl Julius White ....Onancock, Va.

Trade Teaching

*Walter James Atkins ....Newport News, Va.
*Charles Cabell Carter ....Huntington, W. Va.
*Isaac Edward Caster ....New York, N. Y.
*Alfred Philander Farmer, Jr. ....Evansville, Ind.
*Samuel Benard Peterson ....Hockessin, Del.
*Robert Fabian Short ....Baltimore, Md.
*Henry Williams ....Greenwood, S. C.

Candidate for Diploma in THREE-YEAR COURSE

School of Nursing

*Lula Catherine Jordan ....Newport News, Va.

Candidates for Diplomas in TWO-YEAR COURSES

School of Education

Dorothy Virginia Brown ....Roanoke, Va.
Hattie Elise Brown ....Portsmouth, Va.
Ursula Sheppard Colding ....Norfolk, Va.
LaPerle K. Bridges Flack ....Knoxville, Tenn.
Lydia Greenhow Hall ....Norfolk, Va.
Nannie Elizabeth Harrison ....Phoebus, Va.
Lucy S. Herring ....Lillington, N. C.
Hattie B. Manning Hicks ....Norfolk, Va.
Carrie Montgomery Higgs ....Nandua, Va.
Mary Charlton Holliday ....Statesville, N. C.
Vynetta Harriett Ingram ....Newport News, Va.
Susie G. Johnson ....Franklin, Va.
Annie Elizabeth Edwards King ....Washington, D. C.
*Mary Elizabeth Knight ....Robersonville, N. C.
Gertrude Venable Medley ....Hampton, Va.
Drucilla Lushington Moultrie ....Lynchburg, Va.
Alice White Murphy ....Portsmouth, Va.
Louise S. Myers ....Phoebus, Va.
Nettie Louise Riddick ....Norfolk, Va.
Geneva Cornwell Scott ....Newport News, Va.
Calista Virginia Sheppard ....Norfolk, Va.
Jettie Vera Summersett ....Whiteville, N. C.
Rita Verna Watkins ....Newport News, Va.
Sadie Thomaseane Wilson ....Roxbury, Va.

Candidate for DIPLOMA

HAMPTON TRAINING SCHOOL FOR NURSES

Hazel Leona Hairston ....Davy, W. Va.

---

*On completion of work during the summer.

65

Candidates for DIPLOMAS

THE TRADE SCHOOL

Diploma with Distinction

Philip Hosea Demosthenes Chapman

Philip Hosea Demosthenes Chapman	Tailoring	Wilmington, Del.
Scipio Henry Collins	Painting	Savannah, Ga.
Samuel William Dowtin	Printing	Wise, N. C.
Capers James Dunmore	Carpentry	Georgetown, S. C.
James Theodore Henderson	Bricklaying	Portsmouth, Va.
Nathan Paul Hill	Automobile Mechanics	Far Rockaway, N. Y.
Lucas Jackson Howard	Automobile Mechanics	Wilmington, N. C.
Aldrich Hill Jackson	Tailoring	Charlottesville, Va.
Junius Lee Thomas Jeffries	Carpentry	West Point, Va.
Clarence Hugo Jones	Printing	Leesburg, Fla.
Kenneth Odell Jones	Printing	Blenheim, Va.
Charles Wilbert Maddux	Automobile Mechanics	Greenville, Ga.
Nelson Ralph Nance	Automobile Mechanics	Knoxville, Tenn.
Enoch Luehasue Nixon	Bricklaying	Scotts Hill, N. C.
Day Fugad Reed	Printing	Elkhorn, W. Va.
Jerry Miah Ross	Cabinetmaking	Danville, Ky.
Clifton Ulysses Scott	Carpentry	Baltimore, Md.
Ora Webster Spady	Carpentry	Seaview, Va.
Nero White Toney	Carpentry	Winston-Salem, N. C.
John Harold Washington	Printing	Bessemer, Ala.
Charles Burrus Franklin White	Printing	Washington, D. C.
William Kaleb Young	Bricklaying	Asheville, N. C.

ALMA MATER SONG

1. O Hampton, a tho't sent from heaven above,
   To be a great soul's inspiration;
   We sing thee the earnest of broad human love,
   The shrine of our heart's adoration;
   Thy foundation firm and thy roof tree outspread,
   And thy sacred altar fires burning,
   The sea circling round thee soft skies over head.
   Dear Hampton, the goal of our yearning.

Chorus:
   O Hampton, we never can make thee a song,
   Except as our lives do the singing;
   In service that will thy great spirit prolong,
   And send it thro' centuries ringing.

2. Kind mother, we'll treasure the dear happy days,
   We've spent here in life's preparation;
   Yet go with brave hearts upon our chosen ways,
   Of service of God and our nation;
   Still wearing our colors the blue and the white,
   As pledge that our fond hearts will cherish,
   A love which for thee ever shines true and bright.
   A loyalty that ne'er can perish.

The Sixty-fifth Commencement

of

Hampton Institute

OGDEN HALL

Wednesday afternoon, May 29, 1935, at 2:15 o'clock

Program

Invocation   REV. S. ARTHUR DEVAN

The Heavens Are Declaring   *Beethoven*

1. The heavens are declaring the Lord's
endless glory;
Through all the earth His praise is
found.
The seas re-echo the marvelous story,
O man, repeat that glorious sound.
The starry host He orders and
measures,
He fills the morning's golden springs;
He wakes the sun from his night-
curtained slumbers;
O man, adore the King of kings,
O man, adore the King of kings.

2. What power and splendor, and
wisdom and order,
In nature's mighty plan unrolled!
Thro' space and time to infinity's
border,
What wonders vast and manifold!
The earth is His and the heavens
o'er it bending,
The Maker in His works behold;
He is, and will be, through ages
unending,
A God of strength and love untold,
A God of strength and love untold.

AUDIENCE

Address   DR. FREDERICK D. PATTERSON
                                        President-elect of Tuskegee Institute

I Am Seekin' For A City

AUDIENCE, (standing) led by Wilhelmina A. Porter '33

Presentation of Prizes

Albert Howe Prize in Agriculture
The James E. Gregg Prizes
The George Foster Peabody Prize
The Holmes Music Trophy

Announcement of The Merrick-Moore Memorial Scholarship

Conferring of Diplomas and Degrees

PRESIDENT ARTHUR HOWE

Alma Mater Song (Words are printed on the last page)

The audience will please stand both as the procession enters and as it leaves the hall.

* * * * *

Immediately after the exercises the audience is invited to the ceremony of "Retreat", which will be held on the church lawn.

ORDER OF THE ACADEMIC PROCESSION
Marshal
President and Speaker of the Day
Chaplain, Trustees, President of Alumni Association
Directors of the Schools
Administrative and Educational Boards
Assistant Marshals
College and Phenix School Faculties
Trade School Faculty
Alumni
and the following
(by degree and diploma groups according to height)

CANDIDATES for DEGREES and DIPLOMAS
THE COLLEGE

Candidates for Degree of MASTER OF ARTS

Sanford Pearl Bradby   Aiken, S. C.
    B. S., Hampton Institute, 1930
Purvis John Chesson   Norfolk, Va.
    B. S., Commerce, Howard University, 1923
Allen Quinn Jones   Gainsville, Fla.
    B. S., Florida Agricultural and Mechanical College, 1915
Oliver T. Robinson   Henderson, N. C.
    A. B., Knoxville College, 1923

Candidates for Degree of BACHELOR OF SCIENCE

DEGREE WITH HIGHEST HONORS—Jane Eliza Tuitt
DEGREE WITH HONORS—Janie Matilda Mann
Lillian E. Paxton
Lowell Cofield Tilry

School of Agriculture

Maurice Wilbur Coleman ....Blantons, Va.
*Thomas Joseph Culler ....Fort Valley, Ga.
Leonard Alexander Johnson ....LaGrange, La.
Thomas Edward Johnson ....Centreville, Md.
Joseph Thornton Smith ....Kansas City, Mo.

School of Business

Lois Velma Anderson ....Pine Bluff, Ark.
Lawrence Liston Baylor ....Washington, D. C.
Matthew Frank Bland ....Disputanta, Va.
Benjamin Brady Booker ....McKeesport, Pa.
Lawrence Immanuel Brockenbury ....Milford, Conn.
Mattie Davis Clarke ....Phoebus, Va.
Margaret Elizabeth Fonvielle ....Norfolk, Va.
Ellen Burnette Hill ....Hampton, Va.
Russell Charles Hunter ....Cleveland, O.
Helen Amelia Johns ....Lynchburg, Va.
Harold William Powers ....Westfield, Mass.
Blanche Corinne Wyche ....Waverly, Va.

School of Education

Constance Gertrude Adams ....Watsontown, Pa.
Claude Weaver Anderson ....Zanesville, O.
Eugenia Byrd Baptist ....Newport News, Va.
Grace Verdelle Baptist ....Newport News, Va.
Ada Gertrude Battle ....Clinton, N. C.
William Albert Bell ....St. Louis, Mo.
*Marjorie Johnson Bland ....Farmville, Va.
Empsie Taylor Botts ....Hampton, Va.
Juanita Portia Burgess ....Orangeburg, S. C.
Margaret Elizabeth Butler ....Charlotte Hall, Md.
Henry David Carpenter, Jr. ....Louisville, Ky.
Charles Herbert Clark ....Cheneyville, La.
William Henry Neal Cooper ....Marion Station, Md.
Thelma Louise Duncan ....Hampton, Va.
Burner Dean Foster ....Lincoln, Ill.
Eula Earl Hackley ....Roanoke, Va.
Nettie Lucille Hackley ....Roanoke, Va.
John Harrison Hector ....Eustis, Fla.
Mary Deane Johnson ....Hewlett, N. Y.
Melvin Earl Johnson ....Binghamton, N. Y.
Anna Elizabeth Jones ....Lancaster, Ky.
James Alvin Jones, Jr. ....Baltimore, Md.
*Margaret Cornick Lamb ....Norfolk, Va.
Earl William Lewis ....Pittsburgh, Pa.
James Frank Martin ....Leaksville, N. C.
William Cornelius Nixon ....Baltimore, Md.
Randall Gilbert Parker, Jr. ....Philadelphia, Pa.
Lillian E. Paxton ....Roanoke, Va.
James Hubert Penn ....Winston-Salem, N. C.
Ora Lee Pipkin ....McCall, S. C.
Mary Elizabeth Poole ....Norfolk, Va.
Archene Imogene Quinn ....St. Louis, Mo.
Mary Letitia Richards ....Roanoke, Va.
Tamah Zenobia Richardson ....Hampton, Va.
Annie Lee Rivers ....Lawrenceville, Va.
Visel Savage ....Hampton, Va.
*Neider Edlow Simpson ....Newport News, Va.
Lola Cofield Tilly ....Oklahoma City, Okla.
Lowell Cofield Tilly ....Oklahoma City, Okla.
Jane Eliza Tuitt ....Christiansted, V. I.
Josie Mabel Wells ....Rocky Mount, N. C.
Alonzo Ernest White ....Philadelphia, Pa.
Ethel Elenor White ....Lynchburg, Va.
Janarah Gwendolyn Williams ....Wilmington, N. C.
St. John Williamson ....Neches, Tex.
*Joseph Alexander Wiseman ....Annapolis, Md.
Merritt Webster Wilson ....Philadelphia, Pa.

School of Home Economics

Natalie Frances Butler ....Washington, D. C.
Mae Emma Finch ....Paris, Ky.
Elizabeth Hall ....Lynchburg, Va.
Lucille Marian Hayes.................................Tuskegee Institute, Ala.
Kizzie Ann Hewlett ....Richmond, Va.
Emma Frances Hillian ....Hamlet, N. C.
Bertha Lee Holder ....Whistler, Ala.
Emmy Garvin Hunt ....Downingtown, Pa.
Edris Malinda Jackson ....Raleigh, N. C.
Ida Eliza Katherine Jones ....Coatesville, Pa.
Mattie Emma Pegues ....Darlington, S. C.
Lulu Belle Pruitt ....Florence, Ala.

Clara Eugenia Majors Seay .... Lynchburg, Va.
Clumpertee Pretlo Taylor .... Fitzhugh, Ga.

Library School

Esther Mary Crenshaw .... Xenia, O.
    B. S., Wilberforce University, 1933
Hazel Celestine Edwards .... Thomasville, Ga.
    A. B., Talladega College, 1927
Julia Emerson James .... Durham, N. C.
    A. B., West Virginia State College, 1930
Jane Harris Jason .... Corozal, P. R.
    B. S., Hampton Institute, 1932
Alma Isabella Morrow .... Greensboro, N. C.
    A. B., Howard University, 1924
Frank Mancefield Nelson .... Atlanta, Ga.
    B. A., Morris Brown University, 1931
Johnnie Mae Elaine Newton .... Houston, Tex.
    B. A., Fisk University, 1931
Athelma Rogers Nix .... Orangeburg, S. C.
    B. S., State Agricultural and Mechanical College, S. C., 1933
Martha Darwin Roney .... Indianapolis, Ind.
    A. B., Indiana Central College, 1933
Agnes M. M. Scott .... Atlanta, Ga.
    A. B., Atlanta University, 1931
Mabel Louise Seate .... Durham, N. C.
    A. B., North Carolina College for Negroes, 1934
Dorothy Mae Shepard .... Durham, N. C.
    B. A., Fisk University, 1930
Irene Celeste Watson .... Washington, D. C.
    B. S., Miner Teachers College, 1934
Mildred Christine Carey .... Charlottesville, Va.
Lillie Katrena Daly .... Montgomery, Ala.

School of Music

Wallace Jeremiah Campbell .... Hartsville, S. C.
Viola Mabel Coleman .... Roanoke, Va.
Mary Alice Virginia Henderson .... Charlottesville, Va.
Iona Elaine Johnson .... Laurinburg, N. C.
Ethel Leola Lawrence .... Newport News, Va.
Janie Matilda Mann .... Phoebus, Va.
Noah Francis Ryder .... Cincinnati, O.
Catherine Christine Spencer .... Roanoke, Va.
Mary Lee Shuford .... Hickory, N. C.
Flora Elizabeth Thorpe .... Cincinnati, O.
Annette Elizabeth Whitehead .... Bluefield, W. Va.

Trade School

Building Construction

Richard White Adams .... Denver, Colo.
Haywood Augustus Clay, Jr. .... Richmond, Va.
Luther William Hatcher .... Kansas City, Mo.
Henry Lewis Livas .... Paris, Ky.
Frissell Clifton Walker .... Phoebus, Va.
Anthony Daniel Watson, Jr. .... Fort Valley, Ga.
Robert Emanuel Webber .... Brunswick, Ga.
Blake Meriweather Williams .... Asheville, N. C.

Trade Teaching

*Ellis Roland Deans .... Portsmouth, Va.
*William Kaleb Young .... Asheville, N. C.

Candidates for Diplomas in THREE-YEAR COURSE

School of Nursing

*Nita Lourine Allen .... Newport News, Va.
*Dorothy Anne Dudley .... Frogmore, S. C.
*Lois Margaret Harmon .... Washington, Ind.
*Elva Jane Whittle .... Hampton Institute, Va.

Candidates for Diplomas in TWO-YEAR COURSE

School of Education

Hallie Traynham Benjamin .... Capeville, Va.
Hattie H. W. Boaz .... Hampton, Va.
Ethel Louise Bradby .... Newport News, Va.
Annie O. Waters Brown .... Pocomoke, Md.
Carloza Beatrice Clayton .... Newport News, Va.
Ocie B. Cooke .... Newport News, Va.
Olivia Beatrice Edwards .... Yorktown, Va.
Annie House Gaston .... Phoebus, Va.
Anna Smith Holmes .... Lynchburg, Va.
Wilma B. Johns .... Portsmouth, Va.
Sadie Roberta Nelson .... Hampton Institute, Va.
Ethel Sherid Parker .... Portsmouth, Va.
Freda Estella Randall .... Hornsbyville, Va.
Hermione Virginia Smith .... Lynchburg, Va.
Lula Virginia Stewart .... Lynchburg, Va.
Rowena Hodges Towe .... Norfolk, Va.
Coma Porter Walden .... Holland, Va.
Ellen Lewis Whitlock .... Danville, Va.
Susie Agnes Wiggins .... Newport News, Va.
Vera Marcelle Wilson .... Keysville, Va.

*Subject to completion of work during the Summer of 1935

THE TRADE SCHOOL
Candidates for DIPLOMAS

Lloyd Albert Austin ....Printing .... Buchanan, Va.
Walter Clinton Briggs ....Tailoring .... Normal, Ala.
Nelson Washington Bryan ....Tailoring .... Beaufort, S. C.
Samuel Arthur Bryan, Jr. ....Printing .... Beaufort, S. C.
Edward Daniel Carpenter ......Painting .... Rock Castle, Va.
Alfonso Chisholm ....Automobile Mechanics .... Rock Hill, S. C.
George Nelson Davis ....Electricity .... New Castle, Pa.
James Irvin Dennis, Jr. ....Automobile Mechanics .... Princess Anne, Md.
William Henry Fulford ....Bricklaying and Plastering .... Ballston, Va.
*Joseph Harold Fuller ....Bricklaying and Plastering .... Fort Valley, Ga.
Jacob Mack Gamble ....Bricklaying and Plastering .... Manning, S. C.
Harold Oglethorpe Greene ......Electricity .... Beaufort, S. C.
Alphonso Griffin ....Sheet Metal Work .... Washington, D. C.
Rufus Virgil Grigsby ....Painting .... Chappells, S. C.
George Freeman Hamilton .....Automobile Mechanics .... Washington, D. C.
Robert Samuel Hamilton ....Automobile Mechanics .... Washington, D. C.
Rendall Burnett Haywood .....Automobile Mechanics .... Baltimore, Md.
Reginald Atlebert Jackson ......Electricity .... Washington, D. C.
Charles Royal Jaymes, Jr. ....Printing .... Washington, D. C.
Ferdinand Vivian Johnson ......Carpentry .... Louisville, Ky.
Henry Lee Johnson ....Painting .... Smithfield, Va.
James Cleveland Jones ....Carpentry .... Amber, Pa.
Hamilton Gregory Kiah ......Automobile Mechanics ...... Princess Anne, Md.
James Edward Knox ....Automobile Mechanics .... Bristow, Okla.
Milton Clarence Lewis ....Bricklaying and Plastering .... Covington, Va.
Julian Harte Lipscombe ....Steamfitting and Plumbing ...... Asheville, N. C.
George Lincoln Lucas ....Machine Work ....Washington, D. C.
Robert Hill Murchison, Jr. ....Automobile Mechanics .... Fayetteville, N. C.
Charles William Pearcy ....Cabinetmaking .... Knoxville, Tenn.
William Chisolm Peddrew ....Steamfitting and Plumbing .... Summerville, S. C.
William Welford Ricks ....Automobile Mechanics .... Anacostia, D. C.
Colonial Washington Robinson ..Automobile Mechanics .... Cape Charles, Va.
George Henry Robinson ....Carpentry .... Kittanning, Pa.
Charles Callaway Ross ....Painting .... Ashland, Ky.
Hige Russell, Jr. ....Carpentry .... Elgin, Tex.
Willis Elmer Sawyer ....Automobile Mechanics .... New York, N. Y.
Herman Clifford Scott ....Tailoring .... Plainfield, N. J.
William Garwood Thompson ....Automobile Mechanics .... Burlington, N. C.
Wilfred Junius Walker ....Bricklaying and Plastering .... Manning, S. C.
Robert Cleveland Waters ....Bricklaying and Plastering .... Washington, D. C.
Rufus Conrad Wright, Jr. ....Automobile Mechanics .... Chicago, Ill.

ALMA MATER SONG

1. O Hampton, a tho't sent from heaven above,
    To be a great soul's inspiration;
    We sing thee the earnest of broad human love,
    The shrine of our heart's adoration;
    Thy foundation firm and thy roof tree outspread,
    And thy sacred altar fires burning,
    The sea circling round thee soft skies over head.
    Dear Hampton, the goal of our yearning.

Chorus:

    O Hampton, we never can make thee a song,
    Except as our lives do the singing;
    In service that will thy great spirit prolong,
    And send it thro' centuries ringing.

2. Kind mother, we'll treasure the dear happy days,
    We've spent here in life's preparation;
    Yet go with brave hearts upon our chosen ways,
    Of service of God and our nation;
    Still wearing our colors the blue and the white,
    As pledge that our fond hearts will cherish,
    A love which for thee ever shines true and bright.
    A loyalty that ne'er can perish.

MORE OPPORTUNITY FOR VOCATIONAL EDUCATION

Mr. Thornton W. Roberts joined the Lincoln Faculty in 1941-1942 school year as D.C.T. Coordinator. He was the first trades instructor. He was very enthusiastic, efficient and a relentless agitator for vocational training in Lincoln. When building space was at a premium, he gave his time and energy with the cooperation of the principal and County Board of Public Instruction for several years and built additions to the old vocational wood shop and other additions about the school to make it possible to give instruction or to begin instruction in carpentry, cabinet work, tailoring, agriculture, typewriting and business and auto-mechanics. The typewriting class had its beginning when the elementary school or grades were on double session permitting Mrs. Terrecita E. Pinder, one of the double session teachers to instruct a class in typewriting in her third grade room in the afternoon session. This was during World War I when it was difficult to procure any kind of equipment. As a beginning, I permitted the use of my office typewriter for instructional purposes. The teacher used her personal portable machine. The few students taking the course were required to pay a fee for the use of the four or five typewriters. These fees created a fund along with money raised from other sources made it possible to buy old used re-conditioned machines.

Mr. Roberts assisted in the preparation for space to inaugurate cafeteria service and renovations in the homemaking room. Incidentally, his wife, Mrs. Maggie Roberts was the first Lunch Room Manager and seller of school lunches from a Concession Stand in the corridor before a room was used and a cafeteria was built. He rendered valuable service as a consultant in the planning for the Industrial Building at the New Lincoln High School.

MUSIC INSTRUCTION SINCE 1946-1947

It has been stated that it was not until the 1946-47 school term that special music teachers were added to the Lincoln Faculty. Miss Lorraine D. Hawkins instructed music in the Elementary and Junior High School while Mr. Jerry C. Miller was the instructor of Band

Instrumentation in the high school and taught mathematics. It was during this time that the groundwork for a band was laid. Mr. Miller had extensive experience with bands and band work in high schools and college as well as in the army. Miss Naomi Britton served as music teacher in the elementary and high school for a year.

Since the year 1951, these special music teachers instructed music classes including other music groups: Mrs. Wilhelmina W. Johnson, Mrs. Geraldine Y. Miller and Mr. Jerry C. Miller, Director of the Band and head of the Music Department. The Department of Music at this Institution has made an excellent contribution to the cultural advancement of music and the fine arts among the students and the community.

Formerly Lincoln high school

A. QUINN JONES ELEMENTARY SCHOOL

The School Seal Was Designed And Adopted in 1946.

This Seal Was Designed And Adopted in 1946.

COMMENCEMENT ACTIVITIES

APRIL 29 to MAY 6

NINETEEN HUNDRED FORTY-SIX

You are cordially invited to attend all these exercises

CALENDAR

Monday, April 29—8:00 P.M. .... Physical Education Exhibit
Tuesday, April 30—8:00 P.M. .... Elementary School Operetta
"The Maid and the Golden Slipper"
Wednesday, May 1—11:00 A.M. .... Assembly
Thursday, May 2 .... Class Day
11:00 A.M.—Senior Class Exercises
Friday, May 3—
11:00 A.M. .... Sixth Grade Graduating Exercises
9:00 P.M. .... Junior-Senior Prom
Sunday, May 5—3:00 P.M. .... Annual School Sermon
Monday, May 6 .... Commencement Day
8:00 P.M.—Commencement Exercises

ANNUAL SCHOOL SERMON

PROGRAM

Prelude
Processional .... "War March of the Priests" (*Mendelssohn*)
Hymn .... "I Know That My Redeemer Lives" (*Wesley-Handel*)
Scripture Lesson
Invocation and Chant
Anthem .... "Send Out Thy Light" (*Charles Gounod*)
Offertory .... (a) "Blessed Savior" (*Hewitt-Offenbach*)
(b) "Ain'a That Good News" (*Dawson*)
Announcements
Solo .... "The Twenty-Third Psalm" (*Malotte*)
Albert L. Daniels
Annual Sermon .... Reverend D. H. McLean, Pastor
Mt. Pleasant Methodist Church
Anthem .... "O, Divine Redeemer" (*Gounod-Cain*)
Girls' Chorus
Recessional
Benediction

COMMENCEMENT PROGRAM

Theme: His Vision Is Our Challenge.
Prelude
Recessional
Anthem .... "Lift Every Voice and Sing" (*Johnson*)
Invocation
Song .... In the Evening By the Moonlight (*James A. Bland*)
Address of Welcome .... Cora L. Murray
Radio Skit .... "The Life of George Washington Carver"
Senior Class
Address—"The Challenge" .... Helen Bell Brown
Song—"This Is My Country" .... (*Raye-Jacob*)
Presentation of Gift
Presentation of Diplomas
Awards
Announcements
Class Song
Benediction

CANDIDATES FOR DIPLOMAS

Pauline Dorothy Anderson
Frances Lydia Batie
Alphonso Blye
Luewilla Brooks
*Helen Bell Brown
Winfield Broxton
Joanna Coward
Albert Lendgreen Daniels
Minerva Franklin
Carrie Lee Green
Julia Lee George
Gladys Mae Jefferson
Mamie Lee Leath
Theodore Mitchell
*Cora Lee Murray
Rosetta Penny
Mary Evelyn Ramsey
Altamese Reed

Alneta Russ
Rudolph Shipp
Lillie Mae Stephenson
Angie Mae Blye Stitt
*Janie Mae Sturks
Fannie Mae Sylvester
Vera Bell Smith
Erma Dell Thomas
Mary Frances Thomas
Nathaniel Thomas
**Herbert Nathaniel Watson
Mildred Watson
Thelma Watson
Pearl Watson
Mildred Welcome
Andrew James Williams
Mae Alice Williams

CHAPTER IV

EXTENSION AND SUMMER SCHOOL INSTRUCTOR

It was a challenge for me to have been appointed by Dr. J. R. E. Lee, President of Florida A. and M. College to conduct the Extension Class for teachers in the Gainesville Center as one of the instructors for more than a decade, beginning the latter part of the twenties and extending through the thirties. It was during this period that there was a very great need for upgrading the training of teachers generally throughout Florida. Some of the Negro teachers in Alachua County had not completed high school while others had completed high school and junior college and were pursuing these extension in service in winter and Summer school attendance to meet requirements for graduation from college and to qualify for proper teaching certificates in the various fields of teaching. Teachers were cognizant of their needs for improvement and responded enthusiastically to the opportunities offered them. Some teachers sacrificed some necessities of wholesome daily living against a background of poor salaries and short school terms in order to accomplish their objectives.

Bethune-Cookman College through the President, Mrs. Bethune, also offered a challenge to me by appointing me to assist in instruction with Dean James A. Bond, Director of Extension Courses in the area of education. This opportunity was offered during a few winter terms on Saturdays.

A salute goes out to those teachers who had the courage and ambition; patience and endurance; hope and faith to attain their objectives. Many of the teachers in Alachua County survived the 'storm' --- advancing themselves and some represent the best prepared teachers in the county and other have migrated to other sections of the state. Some have reached retirement age or years of service.

Especially do I call to mind a very small group of students whom I tutored privately in an evening class for several terms until they completed their high school courses, and because of their zeal, were accepted for enrollment in undergraduate courses college courses. Finally, I recall two of these students who not only continued to complete requirements for the bachelor's degree but have acquired the master's degree in education, viz: Mrs. Lottie Irvin McPherson and Mrs. Lucille Frasier-Childs. These students paid fees amounting to about a dollar a week for three evenings two hours long. If the walls of Lincoln High School of those days could speak, they would reveal many unheralded stories of heroic deeds and accomplishments of many boys and girls of this community.

I quote the words of Hughes Mears, " Every Child A Gift."

"Though few children are geniuses, all children, I discovered, possess gifts which may become their special distinction. A thousand talents await recognition in the able ones who decline to pull into first place; in the slow workers who eventually do a superior job; in those with special interests beyond school demands, like entomology or stamp collecting; in those with a flair for decoration or design; in the natural house-keeper. The young inventor may be so absolved in his work that he neglects important studies; the skillful user of tools may need adult appreciation to protect him from snobbishness of the book learner, including the teacher."

Responding to the invitation of Dr. W. A. Gray, President of Florida A. and M. College, I accepted an invitation to serve as an instructor in the department of education on the Summer School faculty in 1946. I was assigned to teach undergraduate courses in administration and supervision, adolescent psychology, child psychology and Ethics. This experience was quite rewarding for the majority of the students. In each class was composed of teachers in public school and were making efforts to satisfy requirements for extending teaching certificates and acquiring degrees in education. They were largely an interested, conscientious, enthusiastic, and alert group of individuals.

After having taught students over a period of time, one wonders if objectives and accomplishments have been attained by both the student and the teacher. My evaluation from expressions and statements of satisfaction from students along with a variety of periodic checks, indicated to me a satisfactory amount of information from the courses taught were worthwhile. The opportunity to serve in this capacity was rewarding.

ALCOTE CREDIT UNION

ALCOTE Federal Credit Union operated from 1945 to 1950. The name "ALCOTE" was an abbreviation of Alachua County Teachers. I was elected and served the period of time mentioned above as the president. Mr. Gaston T. Cook was the executive secretary of this organization. It was designed to serve the teachers of this county to save by depositing savings as shares in the institution. Members of this organization could save in interest on loans. It was liquidated because of the lack of interest from the majority of the teachers in this county. White teachers were not a part of a unified teachers' group during this period. About a decade later, the Alachua County Teachers' Credit Union was organized and included all teachers and employees in the county school system. This latter credit union had the full endorsement of the county school administration. The general interracial attitudes and relations have improved and are constantly changing. The organization was liquidated without any outstanding indebtedness. Mr. G. T. Cook, Mrs. J. N. West and other officers were commended for their efficient service rendered in handling the business of the credit union.

CHAPTER V

SCHOOL BOND ELECTION

Because of the success of the Alachua County School Bond Election in 1952, Lincoln along with other schools was allocated funds for building construction. The amount of money involved $2,950,000.

There followed a year of planning for the kind of high school building we should have to meet the need. Some questions arose as to the following:

The location of the administrative suite, its contents, offices, space, occupancy, equipment, etc. questions of a similar nature had to be answered and recommendations made to the architect in reference to what would be included in the entire school plant -- such as classrooms, special rooms, science rooms, homemaking suite, music and band rooms, auditorium, cafeteria, gymnasium, industrial or vocational rooms, playgrounds for physical education and athletics, etc.

The Lincoln High School Faculty utilized the various departmental committees along with other expert consultants working with these committees to find the best answers as to kind of building desired to meet present and future needs and desires.

After the plans of the new Lincoln were completed, it required approximately one year to construct the building.

NEW LINCOLN HIGH SCHOOL
Gainesville, Florida
Ground Breaking Ceremonies
Tuesday, April 5, 1955

PROGRAM

Prelude .... Lincoln High School Band
Directed By Mr. Jerry Miller
Opening Prayer .... Rev. W. M. Murray
The Occasion .... Mr. Paul Peters, Supt. of Public
Instruction (Breaks first ground)

Ground Breaking Follows:

Mr. A. F. Edmunds, Director of Instruction
Mr. Russell Simmons, Assistant Superintendent
Mr. A. Quinn Jones, Principal
Representatives of the County Board
Mr. Harold J. Jones, Supervisor
Representative of the Parent-Teachers Association
Student Council President
Other Visiting Friends

Prayer and Benediction.......... Rev. John L. Wallace, Pastor
Greater Bethel A. M. E. Church
Selection.................................. Lincoln High School Band
Willie Coleman, President of the Student Council, Presiding Master
of Ceremonies

Rev. S. M. Weeks, Pastor of Mt. Pleasant M. E. Church, Citizens Chairman, who headed the campaign to assist in passing the bond for the schools, telegrammed congratulations and his inability to be present because of being engaged in a church religious meeting in New York.

COMMITTEES ON SCHOOL EVALUATION

During the entire year 1952-1953, the Lincoln teachers made a self-evaluation of the school program in its entirety, based on the 1950 Edition of the Evaluative Criteria for Secondary Schools.

Lincoln High School teachers during the 1953-1954 school year were engaged in studying and recommending the kind of building and facilities needed to implement the curriculum for the New Lincoln School scheduled for completion by the 1956-1957 school term.

The following committees of teachers were appointed for the self-evaluation and for making recommendations for the building and facilities.

Consultants worked with these committees:

STEERING COMMITTEE

John Dukes

John Franklin Jones, Sr.
A. Quinn Jones, Prin.
Mrs. I. C. Noble
Mrs. D. A. Duval

EDUCATIONAL NEEDS

R. M. McGhee, Chairman
T. B. McPherson
Mrs. E. V. Heidt
D. A. Roberts
John L. Cook

AGRICULTURE

L. V. Davis, Chairman
N. P. Jackson

PROGRAM OF STUDIES

Mrs. Gloria C. McCoy, Chairman
Mrs. Frederica M. Jones
Miss Wilma P. Holloway
Rayfield M. McGhee
Thornton W. Roberts
Dewey A. Roberts
Learla V. Davis
Mrs. Inez C. Noble
Thomas B. McPherson
Mrs. D. A. Duval

SPANISH

Miss A. H. Fuller
Miss A. B. West

MUSIC

Jerry C. Miller, Chairman
Mrs. Wilhelmina W. Johnson

83

A. Quinn Jones, Sr.

ART-INDUSTRIAL ARTS

Dewey A. Roberts, Chairman

Herman A. Fitz

PUPIL POPULATION

L. V. Davis, Chairman
Miss C. A. Jones
Oliver H. Jones

Miss Louise K. Hill
Miss Inez A. Jackson

ENGLISH

Mrs. Frederica M. Jones, Chairman

Mrs. Ellen V. Heidt
Mrs. Bessie C. Belle
Miss A. H. Fuller
Miss M. A. Melett
Mrs. B. S. Robinson
Miss A. B. West
Mrs. E. A. Glasper
Miss Sarah E. Dubois

MATHEMATICS

Miss Wilmer P. Holloway,
Chairman
Oliver H. Jones

John C. Rawls

PHYSICAL EDUCATION FOR BOYS

T. B. McPherson, Chairman
Robert Acosta
Robert Jones

HEALTH AND SAFETY

Robert Acosta, Chairman
T. B. McPherson
Miss Marion V. Clemons-
Wright
Miss Willie M. McCoy
Mrs. E. L. Patterson

INDUSTRIAL VOCATIONAL EDUCATION

Thornton W. Roberts,
Chairman
Dewey A. Roberts
E. B. Franklin
N. R. Nichols
Herman A. Fitz
Frederick E. Jenkins
Mrs. Pauline E. Trapp-Jones
John L. Cook
Andrew R. Mickle

PHYSICAL EDUCATION FOR GIRLS

T. B. McPherson, Chairman

Mrs. Marion V. Wright Co-
Chairman

Miss Inez A. Jackson
John Dukes
Louis I. Dubois

Miss Willie M. McCoy
Mrs. E. L. Patterson

HOME ECONOMICS

Mrs. Mabel S. Dorsey

Miss Louise K. Hill, Chairman
Mrs. E. I. Hightower

SOCIAL STUDIES

Mrs. Gloria C. McCoy,
Chairman
Robert H. Jones
Mrs. A. C. Nearly
Thomas Coward
Mrs. Carrie B. Lovett
Mrs. E. D. Cook

SCIENCE

R. M. McGhee, Chairman
J. F. Jones
N. P. Jackson
Mrs. Dorothy M. Ham-Yong
Oliver R. Maxey
J. C. Rawls

LIBRARY SCIENCE

Miss Cornelia A. Jones
Mrs. Carrie B. Lovett

PUPIL ACTIVITY

Mrs. D. A. Duval, Chairman
Mrs. A. C. Nealy
Jerry C. Miller
Miss Louise K. Hill
T. B. McPherson

GUIDANCE

Mrs. Anna C. Nealy, Chairman
J. F. Jones
Miss L. K. Hill
R. M. McGhee
Mrs. Mabel H. Dorsey

SCHOOL STAFF AND ADMINISTRATION

A. Quinn Jones, Chairman
Mrs. D. A. Duval
J. Franklin Jones
Mrs. A. C. Nealy

SCHOOL PLANT

Dewey A. Roberts, Chairman
Thornton W. Roberts
L. V. Davis
Herman A. Fitz

STATISTICAL SUMMARY AND GRAPHICS

OLIVER H. JONES, CHAIRMAN
JOHN DUKES
MISS WILMER P. HOLLOWAY

CHAPTER VI

RETIREMENT AND APPRECIATION

I taught as principal under the following County Superintendents:

Mr. E. R. Simmons	Yr.	1921
Mr. Horace F. Zetrouers		1933
Mr. Howard W. Bishop		1941
Mr. Paul Peters		1952
Mr. Edward Manning		1957

It was in March of the 1956-57 school term that I decided to retire from the principalship of Lincoln and as teacher at the close of the school year July the first. This information through Supt. Mannings was conveyed the Trustees and the Alachua County School Board and was approved April 9th. The public announcement of my retirement was published in the *Sunday Morning Daily Sun* March 31, 1957.

Following this announcement, appreciation activities for the retiree began to take various forms.

Sunday, April 14th, 1957, 3:00 P.M., A. Quinn Jones Elementary School presented a program of appreciation in the school auditorium. (see program)

Sunday, May 19th, 4:00 P.M., the Faculty and Students of Lincoln High School presented a program honoring Mr. A. Quinn Jones in the school auditorium and gymnasium. (see program).

PLAQUES, AWARDS, LETTERS, TELEGRAMS, ETC. WERE RECEIVED

Many were the presentations of various kinds were accorded him during the reception and over a period of several weeks

87

culminating at the Lincoln Commencement Program and our trip to Cuba.

It might be of interest to list some of the testimonials.

PLAQUES

The Florida State Teachers Association
Booker T. Washington Plaque for Meritorious Service

*   *   *   *   *

Faculty and Students of Lincoln High School
36 Years of Educational Leadership

*   *   *   *   *

Faculty of A. Quinn Jones Elementary School
Meritorious Service

*   *   *   *   *

Epsilon Pi Lamda Chapter
Alpha Phi Alpha Fraternity
Lifetime of Community Service Devoted to the Cause of Education of Our Youth and the Community at Large. Dec. 8, 1957

*   *   *   *   *

Greater Bethel A. M. E. Church
Service Rendered

*   *   *   *   *

Baratley Temple Methodist Church
Senior Citizen

*   *   *   *   *

Assortments of Jewelry: Ring (Masonic), cuff links, tie clamps, Diamond tipped cuff links and tie clasp

* * * * *

CITATIONS

Alachua County School Board
42, years to the Cause of Public Education. July 1, 1957

* * * * *

Alachua County Teachers Association
In Recognition of Years Service as President

* * * * *

Alachua County Teachers Association
On Becoming Retired

* * * * *

Florida A. and M. University
Meritorious Achievement and Distinguished Service as an effective, successful teacher and Principal and a promoter of Better Community Relationships. Dr. Geo. W. Gore, President. June 3, 1957

* * * * *

Greater Bethel A. M. E. Sunday School
30 years of Meritorious Service as Superintendent of Sunday School

OTHER CITATIONS

The President of the United States of America in Recognition for Service in Connection with the Selective Service Training and Act. December 18, 1943. Franklin D. Roosevelt, President

United States of America Meritorious and Patriotic Service and time given in connection with Price Control and Rationing Program. Harry Truman, President. November 23, 1945

* * * * *

Selective Service as a Member of the Advisory Board for Registrants June 4, 1942 to Feb. 28, 1947

* * * * *

The Vagabond Club for: Deep Appreciation for the People, Untiring Service in Education and Scholarship. L. V. Davis, President. December 17, 1950

LETTERS OF APPRECIATION AND THANKS

Mr. and Mrs. J. B. Carmichael
Citizens Bank of Gainesville. April 2, 1957

* * * * *

Mrs. E. T. Bell
Bell's Nursery
Gainesville. April 8, 1957

* * * * *

Billy Matthews
U. S. Congress
House of Representatives. April 8, 1957

* * * * *

Board of Public Instruction Alachua County
E. D. Manning, Superintendent. April 15, 1957

* * * * *

W. E. Combs, Specialist in Secondary Education
State Department of Education, Tallahassee, Florida, April 12, 1957

*   *   *   *   *

Paul E. Peters, Ex-Superintendent of Public Instruction
Alachua County. June 3, 1957

*   *   *   *   *

Dr. G. L. Porter, Executive Secretary
Florida State Teachers Association. April 14, 1957

Congratulations: My sister Mrs. Hester B. Daughtry Jacksonville, Florida	Congratulations: My Sister Mrs. Josie J. Blackston Jacksonville, Florida
Florida State Department of Education Compliments from Dr. D. E. Williams General Consultant in Instruction May 7, 1957	Congratulations: Fessenden High School O. W. Nealy, Principal May 17, 1957

*   *   *   *   *   *

Congratulations: Quinn, Jr., Glovine & Children	Congratulations: Oliver, Juanita & Children

*   *   *   *   *   *

Congratulations:
Lydia, Ulysses & Boys

A Message From Ernestine Hayes Alexander Dorchester, Mass.	Best Wishes Mrs. Lillie Mitchem

A. Quinn Jones, Sr.

* * *   * * *

Alachua County Vocational
School
Eugene Pullen, Director
Congratulations, May 16, 1957

Madison Street Elementary
School
Students and Faculty
Mrs. Lillian F. Bryant, Principal
May 14, 1957

* * *

Florida A. and M. University
School of Engineering and
Mechanical Arts
M.S. Thomas, Dean, May 16,
1957

CONGRATULATIONS

Sally Ann Duval, Gainesville
Mrs. D. A. Duval, Gainesville
Utopia Bridge Club, Ocala

The Visionaires Club

Mrs. Helen D. Long, Palatka
Lincoln High School P. T. A.
Officers of Greater Bethel A. M.
E. Church

* * *

New Home Makers of America,

* * *

Lincoln Chapter

Vera, Arnette, and the Children

* * *

* * *

Lincoln High School Alumni
Association

May 28, 1957
TESTIMONIAL BANQUET
BY
LINCOLN HIGH SCHOOL

Income:	45 Teachers Paid	$10.00 each	$450.00
Expenditures:	Happy Holiday Vacation to Cuba		$244.48
	Tea		76.01
	Programs		32.35
	Decorations		15.00
	Picture Frame	$5.13	
	Photographer	8.00	
	Student Council	2.95	16.08
Miscellaneous:			
	Labor	$2.00	
	Gas	1.00	
	Stamps	4.50	
	Ice	.35	7.85
Invitations			7.47
Orchid			4.50
			$403.74

Expense check to Mr. A. Q. Jones

	Taxi Fares	
	Cuban Tax	
	Meals during Travel	
	et Cetera	$46.16
	Cost of Check	.10

Submitted by Mr. A. R. Mickle
Lincoln High School Students presented luggage for me to make the trip to Cuba

* * * * * * *

Mr. A. QUINN JONES IN RETIREMENT
Congratulations
Delta Sigma Theta Chapter
Zeta Phi Beta Sorority
Culture, Idealism, Service
Education, Leadership, Loyalty
1958

* * * * * * *

Many and varied were the acts of appreciation extended me as I retired but I should think that the all-expense trip given to me and Mrs. Jones to Cuba by the Lincoln High School teachers was the capstone to the testimonials that I received. We left Jacksonville by Eastern AirLine Plane the morning of July first 1957. In about an hour and one-half we arrived in Havana after having made a brief stop and change of planes in Miami. The tour included many scenic spots in Old and New Havana as well as the 300 year old Morro Castle on the Gulf of Mexico. Our headquarters while in Havana was at the Hotel Lincoln. We returned from our trip on July the fourth.

I acknowledge with deep appreciation and gratitude the many gifts, cards, telegrams, flowers, letters, and other expressions. These courtesies will never be forgotten.

Lincoln High School's Thirty-third Commencement Exercises May 31, 1957 culminated the school activities of the current year but also a period of thirty-six years of continuous educational service to Gainesville and Alachua County and a total of forty-two years teaching in Florida.

The Annual School Sermon was delivered by Dr. G. W. Washington, Pastor of St. Paul C. M. E. Church, Gainesville, Sunday May 26, 3:00 P. M.

The Commencement Address was delivered by Reverend M. G. Miles, Director of Student Activities, Florida A. and M. University. A class of eighty-five received diplomas from Principal Jones with the authority from the Alachua County Board of Public Instruction.

BRIEF HISTORICAL BACKGROUND

Lincoln High School was preceded by Union Academy which was located on the grounds of the present Recreation Center at the corner of North West Second Street and Sixth Avenue. It was a two-story wood building containing eleven rooms and when it was remodeled in 1898, it was worth about $6,000. It was organized in 1866 under the auspices of the Freedman's Bureau, but afterwards came under the control of the Alachua County School Board. In 1897, two years of junior high school work above the eighth grade became a part of the curriculum of the institution.

In 1923, the school moved into a new building located at Northwest Tenth Street and Seventh Avenue, comprising ten acres which the Alachua County School Board purchased from Dr. R. B. Ayer, a parent and prominent civic leader in the Negro community. It is now the site of the A. Quinn Jones Elementary School. The building is an imposing two-story brick structure which was built at a cost of $35,000 and contains principal's offices, 16 class rooms, library classroom science room, home economics room, and an auditorium with a seating capacity for 825. This building housed both the elementary and high school classes until about 1950 when seven all contained elementary classrooms were annexed to the building at approximately $58,000. The cafeteria was constructed and occupied in 1955.

Notwithstanding these additions here and the Duval and Williams school areas, double-sessions to care for the children in all grades elementary and high school were necessary, intermittently, over a period of approximately ten years up to the year 1956.

The complete high school curriculum was added to the school course during the 1924-25 school term, when the school graduated its first group of eight graduates at the regular June Commencement in 1925 as has been stated elsewhere.

In 1925-26, Lincoln High School attained state accreditation by the State Department of Education as the second high school for Negroes to become accredited in the state of Florida. Because of the urgent need for more professionally trained teachers, the State Department of Education authorized Lincoln High School, with the approval of the Alachua County Board of public Instruction, to offer high school teacher training courses as part of high school curriculum for three years, 1928 to 1931. Several of the high school graduates during these three years received Second Grade Teachers Certificates which permitted them to teach in the elementary school grades. Some of them who received these certificates are still employed as teachers in this County.

There were 500 pupils enrolled in grades one through ten at the old Union Academy in 1922 with a faculty of eleven teachers. The high school enrollment increased from 32 students in grades nine through twelve in 1925 with two full-time teachers to 1,000 in the six high school grades in 1956 with a faculty of 50 teachers and other staff personnel.

In September, 1956, the high school moved to the new site at 1001 S. E. Twelfth Street, located on a 53-acre plot of land with the building of concrete and steel construction covering a space of eight acres at a cost of $1,117,000.

LINCOLN HIGH SCHOOL

Located on a 53-acre site the building is of concrete and steel construction and occupies eight acres. The New Lincoln High School plant including equipment cost $1,117,000 and contains:

116,000 square feet of floor space

32 Classrooms

Administrative Wing

Senior Wing

Junior High Wing

Physical Education Wing

Vocational Education Wing

804 Seat Auditorium (Rotunda)

750 Seat Gymnasium 90x120 largest in Florida (Cost of Seats) $8,500.00

Clinic and Recovery Rooms

Teacher Lounges

1,536 Students' lockers, 640 in each HS Wing 250 in Vocational Wing

31 Showers for boys

23 Showers for girls

Band Room with upper-level individual practice booths

Choral Room with upper-level individual practice booths

344-Seat Cafeteria

5 Science laboratories

Book Room

General Purpose Room, Storage Room

Two Libraries

Special wall for outdoor movies (Other facilities include a 60-car paved parking area with a special 7-bus parking space

LINCOLN HIGH SCHOOL GRADUATES 1925 To 1957

School Year	Number
1924-25	8
1926	5
1927	4
1928	5
1929	14
1930	17
1931	9
1932	16
1933	10
1934	50
1935	59
1936	55
1937	22
1938	57
1939	59
1940	37
1941	35
1942	45
1943	56
1944	58
1945	40
1946	56
1947	48
1948	57
1949	41
1950	59
1951	47
1952	55
1953	62
1954	55
1955	58
1956	72
1957	85
Total	1,185

CHAPTER VII

CHURCH MEMBERSHIP

The writer has been a member of the African Methodist Episcopal Church since his infant baptism and a communicant for fifty-seven years. My early Sunday School attendance began at my native hometown Arnett Chapel A. M. E. Church. This reminds me of my remembrance of some of my early Sunday School teachers at this church: Mrs. Alice Rogers, Mr. Charlie Henry, Mr. Duval, and the Superintendent, Mr. John Paramere, who served in this official capacity for quite a number of years. These teachers were present and regular in their attendance on Sundays. There were either teachers whom I do not recall for the moment. Mr. Paramere was consistent in greeting the Sunday School pupils at the church entrance each Sunday morning at 9:30. We were urged to leave home a little earlier, if we were not in time for the opening. When my sister, Josie, became a junior, she was elected secretary of the Sunday School and served for several years under the Superintendency of Mr. Paramere until she moved to Jacksonville, Fla. At one time I was elected a delegate to the Sunday School Convention which convened at Midway, Florida, a rural community in Gadsden County half-way between Quincy and Tallahassee. The horse and wagon was the means for transporting us to the convention . We looked forward to this occasion with great expectations.

It was because of my attendance and instruction in Sunday School that afforded me a greater opportunity to learn Bible Scriptures and teachings and an appreciation for church attendance. These impressions, understandings, and knowledge gained have lingered with me over the years. These early years impressed me to the extent that the few places I have had my residence, have found me a regular attendant of Sunday School and Church services.

When I was principal of the Marianna School, Marianna, Fla. in 1915 and 1916, the Sunday School at St. James A. M. E. Church under the leadership of Rev. N. Z. Graham, the Pastor, was interesting and inviting.

Throughout my tenure as principal of schools at Pensacola, Fla., 1916 to 1921, I maintained regular attendance at Allen Chapel A. M. E. Church both as Sunday School and a regular church communicant. Mr. N. W. Williams was Supt. of Sunday School and Rev. J. A. Brown was pastor for more than a year followed by Rev. C. A. Whitfield.

In another chapter of this compilation, I stated that my membership was transferred to Bethel A. M. E. Church here at Gainesville, Fla., where it has remained since the year 1921. I found that Bethel had been recently re-built under the pastorate of Rev. J. H. Young. Mr. S. L. Redmon was our Superintendent of the Sunday School and remained in this position until about the year 1925. My Class Leader was Mr. Charles Debose who led this class until finally, Mr. Edward Hines was our Leader until his death. I had the opportunity to serve at times as Superintendent of the Sunday School during the pastorate of Rev. H. M. Collins in 1925. He delivered the Annual School Sermon for the first Lincoln High School Graduating Class. He was very prompt and businesslike in his duties. This one thing I experienced that if Sunday School was not dismissed promptly at eleven o'clock in time for beginning the service, he would go in the pulpit and start the service before or in the midst of the Sunday School closing. From that experience, the Sunday School never thereafter extended into the hour for beginning the church service. From this date, from time to time over a period of forty years, I was Superintendent of the Sunday School.

For more than thirty years, I have served on the Trustee Board. The Steward's Board has also claimed some of my time for I remember representing Bethel Church at the District Conference at Citra, Fla. in 1927 during the pastorate of Rev. T. M. White. I have represented Bethel at other District Conferences.

I recall shoveling spades of dirt in preparation for constructing the foundation of Greater Bethel A.M.E. Church the year preceding 1955 when the building was completed during the administration of Rev. J. C. Williams, Pastor.

When I was Superintendent of The Sunday School, a most delightful and rewarding time was spent attending and participating in Sunday School Conventions along with the children selected as delegates. The churches in this district in which conventions have been held are too numerous to mention. However, these are some of the sites where the conventions have been held several times over the years – more than thirty years: Lake Butler, Williston, Bethel and Mt. Olive in Gainesville, Gordon Chapel, Hawthorne, Lacrosse.

It was always an inspiration to attend the State Tri-Meeting at Edward Waters College, Jacksonville. The Special Call Meeting of the General Conference which I attended in Jacksonville in 1958 was impressive. The General Conference which I attended at Los Angeles in 1960 and Cincinnati in 1964 were most rewarding.

It was gratifying to me to share in the spading for the erection of the Church Annex to Bethel and to share in the dedication exercises I 1963 under the pastorate of Rev. Walter S. White.

ADDENDUM

Dr. Oliver H. Jones, son of A. Quinn Jones, will deliver a presentation on September 14, 2003 in the Smathers Library of The University of Florida. The topic of his speech will be an historical review of the legacy of A. Quinn Jones.

This presentation will take place during the weekend of the first football game to be played between Florida A. & M. University and The University of Florida. Until his death in 1997 at the age of 104, A. Quinn Jones was the oldest living graduate of FAMU.

When my father, Dr. Oliver H. Jones, gave the original manuscript of this book to me after my grandfather's death, I cherished and was inspired by all of the valuable information it contained. I was the only grandchild who grew up in Gainesville. I felt compelled to finally have it published in order to share with retired teachers, faculty, principals, former students, the citizens of Gainesville and the world – the full measure of the man named A. Quinn Jones. Having this book published has been a labor of love.

My family members have expanded from working as teachers, librarians, principals, and my father as a Supervisor on the Alachua County School Board, to becoming attorneys, pharmacist, dentist, corporate executives, actress, music/film industry entrepreneur and construction industry entrepreneur.

We are graduates of Howard University, Howard University School of Law, Howard University School of Dentistry, Atlanta University, Edward Waters College, Florida A&M University, Florida A&M University School of Pharmacy, New York University, St. Thomas University School of Law, and in 2007 the University of Concord School of Law.

In the 21st century, the legacy continues.

Sheryle R. Jones
CEO/President
Jones Entertainment Group, Inc.

You are Cordially Invited to be Present at the

Closing Exercises

———OF———

The Quincy Public School No. 1

———

Monday, May 25, 1908, 7:30 P. M.

———AT———

ODD FELLOW'S HALL

Program

SCHOOL MOTTO: To Better the Condition

1 Music, When Visitors Come Round   .   .   .   School
2 Invocation   .   .   .   .   .   Rev. C. A. Whitfield
3 Music, Instrumental Solo, "Whisperings of Love" Kinkel,
　　　　　　Miss Anne B. Kent
4 Welcome Address .   .   .   .   .   .   Mary Jones
5 Words on Welcome   .   .   .   .   Blanche Johnson
6 Paper, Our School .   .   .   .   Mrs. Annie L. Taylor
7 Dialog, ...   "A Slight Mistake"
8 "Willie's Breeches"   .   .   .   .   .   Harry J. Lee
9 Music, Solo, "The Silvery Colorado"   Annie E. Davidson
10 Writing to Grandma   .   .   .   .   Altair U. Hardon
11 Dialog   .   .   .   .   "How The Joke Was Turned"
12 A Story   .   .   .   .   Susie Fields
13 Little Orphant Annie   .   .   .   .   Rossie Masburn
14 Dialog   .   .   .   .   .   .   "The Five Wishers"
15 Little Kittie   .   .   .   .   .   Gertrude Fields
16 Dialog   .   .   .   .   .   .   "The Train to Mauro"
17 When Mother was a Little Girl   .   .   Corine Zieglar

18 Music, Instrumental Solo, . (Selection from Schumann)
Miss Marie E. Hardon

19 March, . . "Little Boy Blue and Little Bo Peep"

20 After Awhile . . . . . . Hattie Preston

21 Dialog . . . . "The Erring Son Reclaimed"

22 Chorus, "Down Where The Daisies Are Blooming" Hart

23 Dialog . . . . . . "The Picnic Party"

24 Columbian Ode . . . . . Mary Holloman

25 A School Girl's Trials . . . . Agnes Campbelle

26 Tambourine Drill . . . . . Sixteen Girls

27 Music, Solo, "Clover Blossoms" . . Fannie Hardon

28 Dialog . . . . "Four Celebrated Characters"

29 Good Night . . . . . Ethyl Fields

30 Remarks by Principal . . . Geo. T. McDaniels

31 Chorus, "Come Smiling Spring" . . . . Tearis

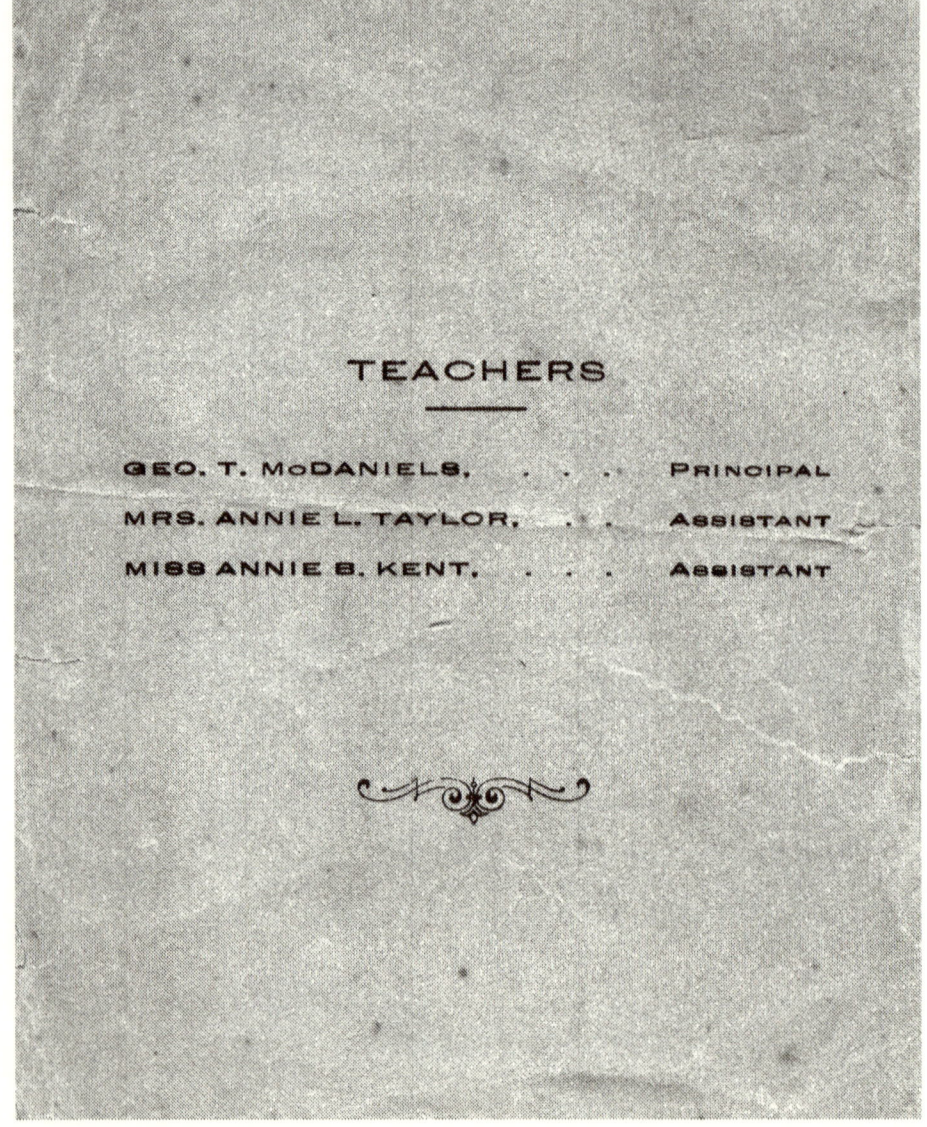

TEACHERS

GEO. T. McDANIELS,	PRINCIPAL
MRS. ANNIE L. TAYLOR,	ASSISTANT
MISS ANNIE B. KENT,	ASSISTANT

Dedication

60

LINCOLN HIGH SCHOOL

SUNDAY, NOVEMBER 18, 1956
3:00 P.M.

Gainesville, Florida

A. QUINN JONES, SR., Principal

Greetings:

The completion of the New Lincoln High School plant marks the beginning of a new epoch in education for the children of Gainesville and Alachua County.

It is with great appreciation that I extend words of commendation to the citizens of Alachua County, the parents and patrons of

the school, the Alachua County Board of Public Instruction, and the Board of School Trustees for the excellent school facilities provided in this building. These facilities will meet the present and growing needs of the children and enhance their learning opportunities.

We are profoundly happy to have you share with us the presentation and dedication of these facilities for the maximum use of our children and for generations to come.

A. Quinn Jones, Principal

C. W. NORTON, *Assistant Principal*

REV. EDDIE J. RIVERS, *Pastor*
Stewart Memorial Methodist Church,
Daytona Beach, Florida

110

LINCOLN HIGH SCHOOL PHILOSOPHY

Lincoln High School believes that education is a life process, which involves the growth of her boys and girls through home, community, and school situations. This school attempts to provide for the life situations of a worthwhile nature, with the view of having its pupils gain experiences which will result in behavior patterns that will enable them to be worthy citizens, living abundantly in our immediate community in particular, and in our country generally.

PROPOSED ALMA MATER

Dear Lincoln High We love Thee
Thy name will ever be,
A song of praise immortal
We pledge our loyalty

Girded with light and knowledge
You brighten up the way
Through strife, defeat, and victory
Honor to Thee we pay.

Hail Alma Mater Hail Thee
Majestic red and white
None greater can transcend Thee
Our love shines pure and bright.

We bow in adoration
And honor to you bring
We shall your name through years defend
In praise to Thee we sing.

Words by G. Y. Fields
Music by Fields and Miller
Arranged by Reid Poole

111

Program

MR. CORNELIUS W. NORTON, Assistant Principal, *Presiding*

Morning Noon and Night Overture..Suppe-Fillmore
　　　　　　Lincoln High School Band, Director, Jerry C. Miller

Processional

How Firm a Foundation..Reading
　　　　　　Audience Standing

Scripture and Invocation..Reverend A. H. Howel

Let Us Now Praise Famous Men..Ralph V. William
　　　　　　Lincoln High School Chorus, Director, Mrs. Geraldine Y. Fields

Introduction of Speaker..Principal A. Quinn Jones

Dedicatory Message..Reverend Eddie J. Rivers, Jr.
　　　　　　　　　　　　　　Pastor, Stewart Memorial Methodist Church
　　　　　　　　　　　　　　Daytona Beach, Florida

No Man Is An Island..Whitney, Kramer, Ringwald
　　　　　　Lincoln High School Chorus

Dedicatory Ceremony: Mr. John C. Rawls, Instructor of Science and Social Studies

　　　　　　　　　　Mrs. Anna C. Nealy, Counselor of Girls

　　　　　　　　　　Mrs. Gloria C. McCoy, Chairman, Department of Social Studies

　　　　　　　　　　Mrs. Mable S. Dorsey, Instructor of Home Making

　　　　　　　　　　Mr. Robert Acosta, Instructor of Physical Education

　　　　　　　　　　Mrs. Daphne A. Duval, Coordinator of Instruction

　　　　　　　　　　Rev. Leroy A. Tillman, President, Parents Teachers Association

Presentation of proposed Alma Mater..Fields-Miller
　　　　　　Lincoln High School Chorus

Greetings:..Mr. Paul E. Fenn
　　　　　　　　　　　　　　Superintendent of Public Instruction

Greetings:..Dr. J. A. Greene
　　　　　　　　　　　　　　Chairman, Alachua County School Board

Greetings:..Mr. Lester Hodge
　　　　　　　　　　　　　　Chairman, Trustee Board

Greetings:..Mr. Don R. Allen
　　　　　　　　　　　　　　Director of Education

Remarks:..Mr. Myrl Hanes

Acknowledgement of Guests and Alumni..Principal A. Quinn Jones

Presentation of Flag..Mr. Frank Roper
　　　　　　　　　　　　　　Commander, American Legion Post No. 16
　　　　　　　　　　　　　　Gainesville, Florida

Battle Hymn of the Republic..Ringwald
　　　　　　Lincoln High School Band and Chorus

Recessional

Benediction..Reverend Leroy A. Tillman

Tour of Building

DEDICATORY CEREMONY

Mr. John C. Rawls:

We have assembled this afternoon in the name of Him who has created all things, and who has given light and life to all mankind for the purpose of dedicating this building. In dedicating this building to the education of our youth, recognize that a good knowledge of the basic skills of reading, writing, and arithmetic is still as highly important today as yesterday. These basic skills are but a part of youth's education. The school must use its power and influence to aid youth in meeting contemporary problems and to help them to live a happy and comfortable life tomorrow. These functions aid in making the school an important institution.

The New Lincoln High School is a well designed and constructed building in which the students may be safe, comfortable and happy. The teachers have the facilities and training to help pupils experience cooperative living; to encourage pride in workmanship so that pupils may have satisfaction from achievement; to open the way for their enjoyment of the arts and a deeper understanding of life; to see that they take part in extra-curricular activities that will add to their learning, social experience, and happiness.

The parents and friends have an institution through which they can feel assured that a definite contribution can be made to the development of our youth's ethical character, It is comparable to good sportsmanship and fair play in athletics; honesty in all school work; respect for property, law and order, and authority; and an attitude of reverence for a Supreme Being.

For a fuller understanding, deeper appreciation and perpetuation of our cultural heritage.
Audience: We dedicate this building.

Mrs. Anna C. Nealy:
For guidance in exploring the fields of human activities preparatory to selecting the right vocation.

Audience: We dedicate this building

Mrs. Gloria C. McCoy:
To lay the foundation for developing the character and skills which merit the full faith and confidence of the various levels of government.

Audience: We dedicate this building

Mrs. Mabel S. Dorsey:
To aid youth in becoming good members of their homes, and understanding the home as a social institution and their place and duties within it.

Audience: We dedicate this building.

Mr. Robert Acosta:
To aid the youth in maintaining personal health and preparing them to participate in, and appreciate the efforts of society as a whole in promoting health and sanitation. To aid the youth in utilizing the resources at their disposal in their own homes and communities for leisure pursuits as found in games, sports, literature, the arts and the sciences.

Audience: We dedicate this building.

Mrs. Daphne A. Duval:
To those persons who ever seek the broadening of mental horizons, the deepening of the wells of knowledge, and the exaltation of scholarship.
In gratitude for the labors of those who planned, and aided in the construction, for those who love and serve this insitution, and in anticipation of the worth to be derived from it.

Audience: We dedicate this building.

Rev. Leroy A. Tillman:
To the glory of God, our Father, by whose favor it has been built; in the honor of Jesus Christ, the Son of the living God our Lord and Savior; to the praise of the Holy Spirit, the source of light and life.

Audience: We dedicate this building.

(Prayer)
Almighty God, unto whom all hearts are open and to Him who knows our vows and gives strength and courage to keep them, we offer ourselves, along with this building. We pray that your eyes be open toward this building day and night; and let your ears be ready toward the prayers of those within its walls. Make us grateful for our heritage, sensitive to our responsibilities, and happy in all of our challenges as we dedicate ourselves to the noble purpose of this building.

121

Compliments Of **ROYAL CLEANERS** Phone FR 6-3131 1001 Northwest 5th Avenue	Compliments Of **J. M. ALDAY PRODUCE, INC.** Wholesale Fruits and Vegetables 115 S.W. 6th St. FR 6-6381	Compliments Of **DUNCAN BROTHERS FUNERAL HOME** 24 Hour Ambulance Service 428 N.W. 8th St. FR 2-9894
Compliments Of **CREVASSE FLORISTS** Phone FR 6-3181 2015 S.E. Hawthorne Rd.	Compliments Of **HOFFMAN PHARMACY** 6 E. Univ. Ave. FR 6-7524	Compliments Of **CAMELLIETTES** Mrs. Mable Dorsey, President
Compliments Of **CLUB COUNCIL** L. V. Davis, President	Compliments Of **JOHNSON'S GARAGE** Hawthorne, Florida Telephone 3531	Compliments Of **JAMES L. STEWARD** Plumbing and Electrical Contractor 611 N.W. 3rd St. FR 2-4594
Compliments Of **MRS. BESSIE M. W. BROWN** Teacher At Lincoln High School 1927-1942	Compliments Of **CLARA'S BEAUTY SALON** Clara, Elouise, and Alice 728 N.W. 7th Ave. FR 6-6338	Compliments Of **THE SANITARY BARBER SHOP** 816 N.W. 5th Avenue
Compliments Of **SARAH'S RESTAURANT** 732 N.W. 5th Avenue Phone 2-9286	Compliments Of **CATO'S SUNDRY SHOP** 737 N.W. 5th Avenue Phone 2-9148	Compliments Of **GREATER BETHEL A.M.E. CHURCH** Rev. A. W. Smith, Pastor
Compliments Of **MT. CARMEL BAPTIST CHURCH** Rev. A. H. Howell, Pastor	Compliments Of **MR. HAROLD J. JONES** Supervisor	Compliments Of **PARKWAY DRIVE IN** Brother Daniels, Prop.
Compliments Of **DR. E. H. DeBOSE** Telephone FR 6-6106	Compliments Of **WALDO ELEMENTARY SCHOOL P.T.A.** Mr. A. Rivers, President	Compliments Of **MUNSON SERVICE STATION** Standard Oil Products Phone FR 2-9049

Compliments Of **THE VAGABOND MEN'S CLUB** L. V. Davis, President	Best Of Luck **RICE'S BICYCLE & KEY SHOP** 101 S.E. 1st St. FR 6-3671	Congratulations **CHESNUT OFFICE EQUIPMENT COMPANY** 106 W. Univ. Ave. FR 2-8421
Compliments Of **BEASLEY & WILLIAMS FURNITURE** 14 S. W. 1st Ave. FR 6-6516	Compliments Of **VISIONNAIRES** Mrs. Viola Jackson, President	Compliments Of **HATCHER'S JEWELERS** 4 E. Univ. Ave. FR 6-6892
Compliments Of **COMMUNITY SHOE SHOP** Oscar Gilbert, Prop. 735 N.W. 5th Ave. FR 2-9354	Compliments Of **PRINCESS BEAUTY SALON** Mrs. Freddie Coles, Prop.	Compliments Of **ST. PAUL C.M.E. CHURCH** Rev. J. B. Bright, Pastor
Compliments Of **HARPER'S DRIVING SCHOOL** "Riding Beats Walking"	Compliments Of **ST. AUGUSTINE CHILD CARE CENTER** Mesdames Harris and Gibson, Teachers	Compliments Of **NEW MARKET** Wayne A. Andrews 427 N.W. 4th St. FR 2-9313
Compliments Of **HAYNES BROS. GROCERY** 747 N.W. 5th Ave. FR 2-9029	Compliments Of **HATTIE'S BEAUTY SHOP** N.W. 10th Street	Compliments Of **FESSENDEN HIGH SCHOOL** Martin, Florida Mr. O. W. Nealy, Principal
Compliments Of **JOHNSON'S GROCERY STORE**	Compliments Of **LINCOLN HIGH SCHOOL LUNCHROOM** Mrs. Jessie Green, Mgr.	Greetings **MAJOR SOCIETY CLUB** Willie Lamar, President
Compliments Of **BI-RITE SUPER MARKET** 1701 Northeast 8th Avenue Phone FR 6-5606	Compliments Of **MT. PLEASANT METHODIST CHURCH**	Compliments of **LINCOLN HIGH QUARTERBACK CLUB** Eugene Mills, President

CONGRATULATIONS

You have our best wishes for many more successful years.

Faculty and Student Body
WALDO ELEMENTARY SCHOOL

J. T. Gaddy, Principal

COMPLIMENTS OF

ROBINSON'S MARKET

Quality Meats and Produce

120 S.W. 1st Ave.   FR 6-6273

Compliments Of

Alachua County
Teacher's Association

MR. I. H. CAFFEY,
President

Compliments Of

Duval Elementary School

"Education does not mean teaching people to know what they do not know; It means teaching them to behave as they do not behave."
. . . RUSKIN

L. M. JACKSON,
Principal

PATRONS

Mrs. E. Acosta
Mrs. Willie B. Aiken
Mr. and Mrs. Dennis Alexander
Mr. and Mrs. Fred Alexander
Mrs. E. Alford
Mr. and Mrs. Collie Allen
Mrs. Marie Armstrong
Mrs. Lorenza Banks
Mrs. Eliza T. Bell
Mr. and Mrs. Willie Bell
Mrs. Lillie Blake
Mrs. Alice Bostick
Mrs. V. V. Bostick
Mrs. L. B. Bradley
Mrs. Terlene Brooks
Mr. A. Brown
Mr. and Mrs. Augustus C. S. Brown
Mrs. Minnie Brown
Miss Ruth Bryant
Mr. and Mrs. Willie D. Burgess
Mrs. Girlie Burns
Mr. and Mrs. Cleo Butler
Mr. and Mrs. I. H. Caffey
Mr. and Mrs. R. C. Cambridge
Mr. and Mrs. Richard H. Carter
Rev. and Mrs. James Cato
Mrs. Mable Cheeseborough
Miss Julia Clemons
Mr. and Mrs. Emmett Coachman
Mr. and Mrs. J. M. Cohen
Rev. and Mrs. L. C. Cohen
Mr. and Mrs. G. T. Cook
Mr. and Mrs. Robert Coleman
Mr. and Mrs. Louis Cook
Mrs. Elizabeth Cooke
Mrs. Julia Cooper
Mr. and Mrs. Jackson C. Crawford
Mrs. Cleo Cunningham
Mr. and Mrs. Robert Daniels
Mr. and Mrs. L. V. Davis and Reggie
Mrs. R. B. Davis
Mrs. Ellen Days
Mr. and Mrs. Primon Dean
Mr. and Mrs. Alec DeBose
Mrs. Bernice DeBose
Dr. and Mrs. E. H. DeBose
Miss Estelle DeBose
Mrs. Sarah DeBose and Daughter
   Dental Clinic
Mr. and Mrs. Joseph C. Dixon
Mr. and Mrs. Arnold Dorsey
Mr. and Mrs. Ernest Dowdell, Sr.
Mr. Luther Dowdell
Mr. and Mrs. Collins Duncan
Miss Dolores Duval
Mr. and Mrs. Archie E. Edwards
Mrs. C. E. Ellis
Mr. and Mrs. Louis English
Mrs. Margaret Evans
Mrs. Kate Ferguson
Dr. Hayden G. Floyd
Rev. H. Foye
Mr. Ed Galloway
Mrs. R. M. Gaskin
Mr. and Mrs. J. T. Gaddy

Mr. and Mrs. Melvin Gillispie
Mr. and Mrs. William S. Glasper
Mr. and Mrs. Fletcher Green
Mr. and Mrs. Morris Green
Mrs. Agnes Gordon
Mr. and Mrs. Cornell Haile
Mr. N. L. Hankerson
Mr. and Mrs. Julius V. Harper
Mr. and Mrs. E. H. Harrison
Mr. E. J. Harrison
Mr. and Mrs. Nathaniel Harrison
Mrs. Edna M. Hart
Mr. and Mrs. S. H. Hendley
Mr. and Mrs. Eddie Henry
Mr. and Mrs. Joseph Hightower, Jr.
Mr. and Mrs. Calvin Hill
Mr. C. Hill
Mr. and Mrs. James Hill
Mrs. E. Hobdy
Miss W. P. Holloway
Rev. and Mrs. A. H. Howell
Mr. and Mrs. Thomas Hurst
Mr. James E. Irvin
Mr. and Mrs. Sam Ivory
Mrs. Sarah Ivory
Miss I. A. Jackson
Mr. and Mrs. L. M. Jackson
Mr. and Mrs. Raford Jackson, Jr.
Miss I. James
Mr. and Mrs. W. L. Jenkins
Miss Lillie Johnson
Mr. and Mrs. Robert Johnson
Mr. and Mrs. Willie L. Johnson
Mr. and Mrs. A. Quinn Jones, Sr.
Mr. Jeff C. Jones
Mr. Johnie Jones
Miss Nancy Jones
Mrs. Thelma M. Jordan
Mrs. Ruby Kimborough
Mrs. Louise Lewis
Mr. and Mrs. K. D. Lovett
Mr. and Mrs. Henry Lloyd
Mr. and Mrs. Booker T. Lyons
Mr. and Mrs. E. E. McAshan
Mrs. Gloria C. McCoy
Mr. and Mrs. Raymond McKnight
Mrs. A. J. McGhee
Miss H. McGhee
Mr. and Mrs. Rayfield McGhee
Miss Verlia Matthews
Miss Willie R. Mazon
Prof. and Mrs. A. L. Mebane
Mrs. H. Metz
Mr. and Mrs. Eugene H. Mills
Mr. and Mrs. Daniel Mitchell
Mr. and Mrs. James Mitchell
Mrs. Fannie Monroe
Mr. Herbert Nattiel
Mr. and Mrs. John L. Neal, Sr.
Prof. and Mrs. C. W. Norton
Mrs. A. M. Palmer
Miss Dalverta Palmer
Mr. James Palmer
Mrs. H. Phillips
Mrs. A. Pridgen

Mr. and Mrs. N. O. Rawls, Sr.
Mr. and Mrs. Monroe Reed
Mr. and Mrs. D. A. Roberts
Mr. Arthur Robinson
Mr. Wm. Blaine Robinson
Mrs. Lucille Robinson
Mrs. M. G. Rudisill
Mrs. F. Sapp
Mr. and Mrs. Stafford Sapp
Mr. and Mrs. J. S. Saunders
Rev. and Mrs. J. S. Shannon
Mr. Dovie Shumake
Mrs. Anna Simmons
Mrs. E. E. Simmons
Rev. and Mrs. W. L. Souder
Mr. and Mrs. Alpha O. Smith
Mrs. Florence W. Smith
Mr. and Mrs. James Smith
Mrs. Mallie J. Smith
Mrs. Maude L. Smith
Mr. and Mrs. Virgil Smith, Sr.
Mrs. Geneva Stafford
Mrs. S. G. Strickland
Mr. L. H. Stroble
Mr. and Mrs. Clifton G. Taylor
Nurse Rosa London Taylor
Rev. E. T. Thomas
Mrs. Fannie Thomas
Mrs. E. Tomlin
Mr. and Mrs. Johnson Trapp
Mrs. Sussie M. Trapp
Mr. and Mrs. Vernon L. Trapp, Sr.
Rev. and Mrs. J. H. Turnipseed
Mr. and Mrs. George Vogt
Mr. Dave Waiders
Mr. Barney M. Walker
Mr. and Mrs. Robert Walker
Rev. and Mrs. E. H. Walker
Mrs. R. W. Walker
Mrs. Martha Warren
Miss H. Wells
Mrs. D. A. Webb
Mr. Leroy Webster
Mr. and Mrs. Furman Welch
Mrs. Jessie N. West
Miss Addie M. White
Mrs. C. J. Wilcox
Miss Harrie L. Williams
Mr. and Mrs. J. W. Williams
Miss Leontine Williams
Mrs. M. Williams
Mrs. M. E. Williams
Mrs. M. H. Williams
Mr. and Mrs. George Williams
Mrs. Rosa Williams
Mr. T. D. Williams
Mrs. L. K. Williams
Mr. Taft Wilson
Mr. Leroy Wims
Mr. and Mrs. F. G. Wingate
Mrs. F. Woods
Mr. and Mrs. Willie Worthy
Mr. and Mrs. Alfred Wright
Rev. and Mrs. George Wright
Mr. and Mrs. Johnny Young

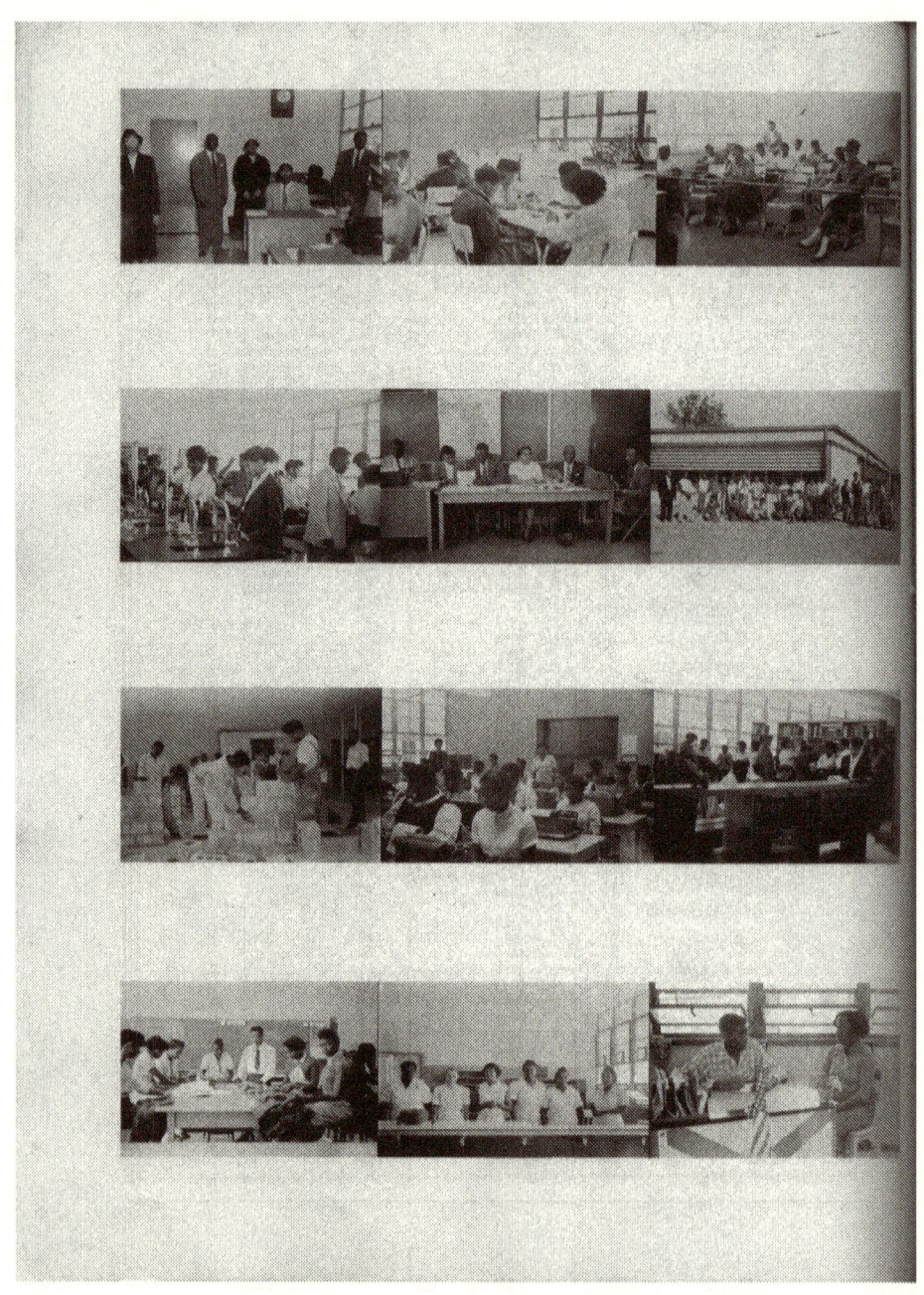

April 14, 1957

A. Quinn Jones Elementary School

presents

Program of Appreciation

Cordially yours, A. Quinn Jones

for

MR. A. QUINN JONES, SR.

PRINCIPAL, LINCOLN HIGH SCHOOL

3:00 P.M.

AUDITORIUM

Mr. JAMES R. GREEN
Principal—Douglas Jr. High School
High Springs, Florida

B.S. DEGREE, F.A.M.U., M.A. DEGREE, HAMPTON INSTITUTE, FURTHER STUDY, MICH. STATE U.

SPEAKER FOR THE OCCASION

CONGRATULATIONS
For Excellent Service Rendered To Humanity
MT. CARMEL BAPTIST CHURCH
A place where you are welcome to worship.
Rev. A. H. Howell—Pastor

CONGRATULATIONS
from
DUVAL ELEMENTARY SCHOOL

"Education does not mean teaching people to know what they do not know; it means teaching them to behave as they do not behave."—Ruskin

L. M. Jackson—Principal

CONGRATULATIONS
In The Field of Education
"Methodist Youth Fellowship"
ST. PAUL C.M.E. CHURCH
Miss Jacquelyn Curington—Pres.   Rev. G. W. Washington—Pastor

---

He has helped the boys and girls in every way
    Now the time has come for his promotion day

He alone deserves the love we can repay
    He helps all the boys and girls be bright and gay

He keeps pace all through each long and crowded day
    He has tried to do his best in his own way

Teachers, students call, and he is always near
    He always says, "I do my best."

Words..............................Mrs. C. L. Henry
To be sung by.......A.Q.J. Teacher Ensemble

THOUGHT FOR TODAY

Give of your best to humanity
Give of your best to all youth
Teach for the love of teaching
Teach what is right and true.

CONGRATULATIONS

FROM

Faculty and Student Body
Lincoln High School

We extend our highest esteem and appreciation to our Principal, Mr. A. Quinn Jones, Sr., for the years of inspired leadership he has given to youth. Many of us have been privileged to receive his guidance both as pupils and teachers. We have always been aware of the high ideals he has maintained for himself and those affiliated witht him.

A TRIBUTE TO AN EDUCATOR, CIVIC AND RELIGIOUS WORKER

Mr. A. Quinn Jones, a Florida product who hails from Quincy, came to Gainesville in 1921, as Principal of Union Academy which at that time went only to tenth grade. It was located at the present site of Carver Library and the Community Recreation Center. In 1923 Mr. Jones moved this school to Old Lincoln High, which now bears his name.

This spontaneous gesture was brought about by the community, alumni and the P. T. A. on his becoming Principal of the New Lincoln High School, from which he will retire this year.

Mr. Jones has been very observant, and through his keen interest for growth and development his school was the second accredited Negro High School in Florida in 1926.

Previous services rendered in the State of Florida as an educator were held at the following posts: Elementary Principal in Gadsden County at Marianna, and at the Elementary and High School in Pensacola. He holds the B.S. Degree from Florida A. & M. University, the Masters Degree from Hampton Institute, with advanced study toward a Doctorate at New York University.

As a civic worker, Mr. Jones affiliated with the following organizations: A member of Greater Bethel A. M. E. Church, Superintendent of the Sunday School for 27 years, Member of the Gainesville Council on Human Relations, Member of the Alpha Phi Alpha Fraternity, Member of Alachua County Teachers Association, Member of the National Association of Secondary Principals, Member of the Association for Supervision and Curriculum Development, Member of the National Association for the Study of Education, Member of the Prince Hall F. A. A. Y. Masons, and Chairman of the Principals' Conference of Alachua County.

Mr. Jones, we salute you on this your day, as we turn with memories of the great deeds of kindness, honesty, and character building of boys and girls throughout the United States. These memories turn with recollection in the lives of youths of America. As the earth rotates on its axis and goes in its obit, swing to planets, so have you helped boys and girls prepare themselves for better service.

When God made man the most important creature on earth he also gave him responsibilities. You have realized your responsibility to man and gave indispensable service to your community. You accepted these things when a boy: "Suffer little children to come unto me, and forbid them not; for of such is the kingdom of heaven." Here as portrayed in this philosophy, in your everyday life, we find you not browsing Sunday's paper or sitting in an easy arm chair on Sunday, but as God abled you to ring a bell at school each day, for your daily bread; the Sabbath found you ringing the bells at church each Sunday morning, bringing classes together by precept and example as Superintendent of your Sunday School. There is no man more loyal than you.

Too much cannot be said of you as a character builder. Your example to boys and girls throughout the state will be remembered as the smiling principal, whose poise and dignity and whose foresight, and culture are beyond comparison. We classify you along with other great men, who appeared to be cast in a greater mould and made of different and finer metal than most men. With your steadfast determination to do your duty at any cost, your nobility of purpose and purity of character makes you loved by all who know you.

The marble stones that mark your production are forty-three (43) years of service as an educator, thirty-six of which were in Gainesville, and four children who are serving in the same categories.

This honor comes to a deserving man, with excerpts spoken by Lincoln:

"Let us do our work well, both the unseen and the seen,

Make the house where gods may dwell, beautiful, entire and clean,

For the structure that we raise time is with material filled;

Our todays and yesterdays are the blocks with which we build."

By

Mrs. F. B. McLendon

E. PLURIBUS UNION um

(One Among Many)

Is

OUR SLOGAN

Of

Congratulations To You

Excelsior Matrons Circle

Mrs. T. M. Jordan, Pres.   Mrs. M. J. Allen, Secretary

EPSILOM PI LOMODA CHAPTER

of

**ALPHA PHI ALPHA
FRATERNITY, INC.**

CONGRATULATIONS

CONGRATULATIONS

We are with you in sports.

QUARTERBACK CLUB

Mr. Eugene Mills, President

Mr. James Hill, Secretary

Mr. F. H. Daniels, Bus. Mgr.

PROGRAM

Song—

Scripture and Prayer..Rev. W. M. Ferguson

The Occasion..Mrs. C. M. Taylor

Selection—Sundown..Ira B. Wilson
    A.Q.J. Teacher's Ensemble (Arrangement of Londonderry Air)

Introduction of Speaker..Principal T. M. Jordan

Address..Mr. James R. Green

Selection..A Tribute
    A. Q. J. Teacher's Ensemble   (Tune—HE)

Presentations
    Plaque To Mr. A. Quinn Jones..Mrs. T. M. Jordan
    Portrait To School

Solo.."Thank God For A Garden"
    Mr. Ammon Jackson

Introductions And Greetings..Mr. Harold Jones
    Supervisor of Negro Instruction, Alachua County

Benediction

Refreshments..Lunch Room
    Mrs. L. V. Davis, Manager

A. Quinn Jones Elementary

CONGRATULATIONS

MR. A. QUINN JONES, SR.

We accept the name of this school with all the honor and dignity shown through your many years of great work.

**FACULTY AND STAFF
A. QUINN JONES ELEMENTARY SCHOOL**

Mrs. T. M. Jordan, Principal

Faculty of A. Quinn Jones Elementary

141

Congratulations
from
SHELL JUNIOR HIGH SCHOOL
for your
Outstanding Educational Work
Eugene E. Mack—Principal

Compliments
of
ROBINSON'S MARKET
Visit this market for fine quality meats and produce.
Phone FR 6-5263

Congratulations And Best Wishes
from
MT. PLEASANT METHODIST CHURCH
The church where there is a pew for you.
Rev. W. Ferguson—Pastor

Congratulations
from
THE CHURCH OF THE KINGDOM OF GOD
Peace! Christ is the answer to all your needs.
Bishop Noah Nothing, Pastor   Prince Phillip Wilcox, Assistant Pastor
402 S.E. 14th Street

Congratulations
from
GREATER BETHEL A.M.E. SUNDAY SCHOOL
Twenty-five years of service in promoting spiritual, moral and
educational values.
Prof. A. Quinn Jones—Supt.   Rev. A. W. Smith—Pastor

Best Wishes Mr. Jones
For twenty-five years of service.
**UINVERSITY CITY LODGE NO. 1218
I.B.P.O.E. of W.**
Fred Alexander, E.R.
Walter J. Coleman, Secretary

A MESSAGE FROM THE BOARD OF PUBLIC INSTRUCTION

We are profoundly happy to congratulate you for your long,
faithful service as principal of Lincoln High School in Alachua County.
We, the members of the Alachua County School Board feel deeply in-
debted to you for your untiring and devoted service.

CONGRATULATIONS FROM PATRONS

Mr. and Mrs. Joseph Acosta
Mrs. Ruby Adams
Mr. and Mrs. C. L. Allen
Mr. Morris Allen
Mr. and Mrs. Dennis Alexander
Mr. and Mrs. Fred Alexander
Deacon and Mrs. Jasper Alexander
Mr. and Mrs. John Alexander
Mr. and Mrs. Hannah Aldridge
   and Family
Rev. and Mrs. Hugh Anderson
Miss Lillie Mae Anderson
Rev. Ashley, Ocala, Florida
Mr. James A. Barton
Mrs. B. Carolyn Belle
Bell's Nursery
Mr. and Mrs. F. B. Blake
Mr. and Mrs. Eugene Brown
Mr. and Mrs Joe Brown
Mrs. Natley Bryant
Mr. and Mrs. James Caldwell
Mrs. Eunice B. Carter
Mr. and Mrs. Willie Coleman
Mr. and Mrs. G. T. Cook
Mr. and Mrs. Louis Cook
Mr. and Mrs. Jackson Crawford
Mrs. Agnes Curington
Mrs. Clyde Daniel
Mrs. Ella Mae Daniel
Mrs. Marie Daniel
Mr. and Mrs. L. V. Davis
Mr. and Mrs. Pirmon Dean
Miss Estelle V. DeBose
Mrs. Bernice DeBose
Mr. and Mrs. Collin Duncan
Mr. and Mrs. Joseph Duncan
Mr. and Mrs. George Edwards
Mr. James Edward
   Hawthorne, Florida
Mr. and Mrs. Ulysees Ellis
Mrs. Margarie Evans
Mrs. Jeraldine Y. Field
Rev. C. F. Ferguson, Sumter, S. C.
Rev. and Mrs. W. M. Ferguson
Mr. Malrice Folsom
   Hawthorne, Florida
Dr. and Mrs. W. A. Gaines
Mr. and Mrs. Edward Galloway
Mr. and Mrs. Wm. Glasper, Sr.
Mr. Dallas Glenn

Mr. and Mrs. Harry Green
Mrs. Minnie Green,
   Supervisor, Marion County
Mr. Roosevelt Green
Mr. and Mrs. Robert Griffin
Mr. Marshall H. Hamilton
Russel and Michael Ham-Ying
Deacon and Mrs. E. H. Harrison
Mrs. Lillian Harvey
Mr. and Mrs. Albert Hendrix
Mr. and Mrs. E. L. Henry
Mr. and Mrs. Thomas Hill
Mr. and Mrs. Joe Hobbs
Mr. and Mrs. Thomas Hurst
Mrs. Lula Hunter
Miss Inez Jackson
Prof. A. O. Jenkins, Starke, Florida
Mrs. Altamease Johnson
Mrs Blanche Johnson
Mr. and Mrs. Joseph Johnson
Mrs. Marie Johnson
Mr. and Mrs. Walter Johnson
Mr. Bobby Jones
Mr. Harold J. Jones
Miss Nancy Jones
Mr. and Mrs. Robert Jones
Mrs. Ellen Jordan
Mrs. Thelma Jordan
Prof. J. Franklin Keller
   Maclenny, Florida
Rev. and Mrs. Henry Kinsey
Deacon J. S. Levette
   Newberry, Florida
Mr. and Mrs. Leroy Lewis
Mrs. Helen D. Long
   Supervisor, Putman County
Mr. and Mrs. Robert E. Love
Mr. and Mrs. K. D. Lovette
Deacon and Mrs. B. T. Lyons
Mrs. G. C. McCoy
Mrs. Flossie B. McLendon
Mr. and Mrs. Henry Miles
Rev. and Mrs. W. A. Miles
Mrs. Gertrude Garmon Moore
   Jacksonville, Florida
Rev. and Mrs. Willie Murray, Sr.
Mr. and Mrs. T. J. Murray
Mr. Willie Murray Jr.
   Detroit, Michigan

Mr. and Mrs. R. M. McGhee
Mr. and Mrs. Daniel Lee Mitchell
Rev. A. A. Mulberry
Mr. John F. Murrell
Mrs. Lizzie Mouzon
   Hawthorne, Florida
Mr. and Mrs. John L. Neal
Mr. and Mrs. C. W. Norton
Mr. and Mrs. Leartice Perry
Mr. Leroy Perry, Miami, Florida
Mr. and Mrs. Charlie Price
Deacon and Mrs. Charles Roberson
Deacon and Mrs. Shelton
   Robinson, Sr.
Mr. Shelton Robinson, Jr.
Mr. and Mrs. William Blaine
   Robinson
Rev. and Mrs. John H. Rowe
   Jacksonville, Florida
Deacon and Mrs. James Sanders
Mrs. Beatrice Scrivens
Mr. and Mrs. J. C. Simmons
Mrs. Hattie Murray Smith
Mr. James Stewart
Rev. and Mrs. W. K. Smith
Deacon and Mrs. Clifton G. Taylor
Mr. and Mrs. James Taylor
Rev. and Mrs. L. A. Tillman
Elder and Mrs. Johnnie Thomas
Mr. and Mrs. Johnson Trapp
Mrs. Susie M. Trapp
Prof. and Mrs. Vernon Trapp
Deacon and Mrs. John Turner
Rev. and Mrs. J. H. Turnipseed
Mr. and Mrs. Frank Vinson
Mr. and Mrs. James A. Walker, Sr.
Mr. and Mrs. Robert H. Walker
Miss Anna Belle West
Mrs. Jessie N. West
Deacon Lorenza Wells
Miss Addie Mae White
Miss Carrie Mae William
Deacon Ed. William
Mrs. Francis William
Mr. and Mrs. George Williams
Mr. and Mrs. Hamp William
Bishop and Mrs. H. William
Lt. and Mrs. Neil Williams
Mr. and Mrs. B. H. Wimby
Rev. and Mrs. George Wright

THE FACULTY AND STUDENTS

of

LINCOLN HIGH SCHOOL

Present a

PROGRAM

Honoring

MR. A. QUINN JONES, SR.

Sunday, May 19, 1957   4:00 P. M.

School Auditorium

— o —

MR. CORNELIUS W. NORTON, ASSISTANT PRINCIPAL, *Presiding*

Prelude

Lead On, O King Eternal ....*Henry Smart*
Audience Standing—(Words on the reverse of this program)

Invocation..REVEREND W. M. FERGUSON
Pastor, Mt. Pleasant Methodist Church

Let Us Now Praise Famous Men..................*R. Vaughn Williams*
Lincoln High School Chorus
Mrs. Geraldine Y. Fields, Directress

The Occasion ....DR. G. L. PORTER
Executive Secretary, Florida State Teachers Association

Greetings—
  Florida State Teachers Association
  Department of Education, State of Florida
  Alachua County Board of Public Instruction
  Lincoln High School Student Body
  Lincoln High School Alumni Association

My Hero ....*Straus-Scotson*
Miss Catherine Berry, Soprano
Mr. Lulius V. Harper, Tenor

Presentations

Let My Soul Rise in Song..*Raymond Rhea*
Lincoln High School Chorus

Benediction..REVEREND LEROY A. TILLMAN
President, Lincoln High School Parent-Teacher Association

(Reception follows immediately in the Charles S. Chestnut Gymnasium)

LEAD ON, O KING ETERNAL

Lead on, O King Eternal,
The day of march has come;
Henceforth in fields of conquest
Thy tents shall be our home;
Thro' days of preparation
Thy grace has made us strong,
And now, O King Eternal,
We lift our battle song.

Lead on, O King Eternal,
We follow, not with fears,
For gladness breaks like morning
Where'er Thy face appears;
Thy cross is lifted o'er us;
We journey in its light;
The crown awaits the conquest;
Lead on, O God of might.

67

LINCOLN HIGH SCHOOL

GAINESVILLE, FLORIDA

Thirty=third

Commencement Exercises

MAY 26 TO MAY 31
NINETEEN HUNDRED FIFTY-SEVEN

SCHOOL AUDITORIUM
A. QUINN JONES, *Principal*

Calendar

Sunday, May 26, 3:00 p.m..Annual School Sermon

Wednesday, May 29, 10:30 a.m...School Assembly
—Awards Program

Thursday, May 30...Class Day
8:00 p.m..Senior Class Exercises

Friday, May 31...Commencement Day
8:00 p.m...Graduating Exercises

Annual School Sermon
Program

Prelude

Processional

Hymn—Dear Lord and Father of Mankind............................Audience

Scripture and Invocation......................................Reverend L. A. Tillman

Chant—Dresden Amen

Anthem—The Heavens are Declaring................................ *Beethoven*

Offertory—Music
1. Good News
2. Jesus Walked this Lonesome Valley
3. Ain'a That Good News

Announcements

Ensemble—The Holy City.................................Weatherly and Adams

Sermon.. Dr. G. W. Washington, Pastor
St. Paul C. M. E. Church

Consecration Prayer

Music—Soon Ah Will Be Done.. *Dawson*

Recessional

Benediction

Commencement Program

Prelude

Processional

God Bless America...Audience

Invocation

Male Ensemble.....................Stouthearted Men—*Romberg-Hammerstein*

Introduction of Speaker

Address...Reverend M. G. Miles
Director of Student Activities
Florida A. and M. University
Tallahassee, Florida

PRESENTATION OF GIFT

PRESENTATION OF DIPLOMAS.................Mr. E. D. Manning, Jr.
Superintendent of Public Instruction

ANNOUNCEMENTS

CLASS SONG

BENEDICTION

Candidates for Diplomas

Walter Eugene Barbour
George Bradley
Winston James Bradley
***Gloria Elaine Brooks
Barbara Ann Britt
Jeraline Bryant
Thelma Lee Burse
***Randolph Elijah Butler
Ethel Louise Campbell
Harold Lee Chisholm
Rudolph Chisholm
Howard James Clark
Luellia Delores Clifton
Leatha Mae Colson
Bobbie Cotman, Jr.
Henry Crosby, Jr.
Jacquelyn Yvonne Curinton
Lottie Marie Danzy
Wilette Annette DeBose
Cora Lee Dickerson
Nathaniel Edward Douglas
Charles Theodis Dowdell
Willie Eugene Dukes
Theodis Eugene Ellis
Tom Fayson
George Dewayne Gibson
Glenn Gilchrist
Walter Harvey Gillespie
Wilford Anthony Griffin
Daisy Mae Haile
Mable Harris
Willie Mae Hartzog
Vernon Wiley Hayes
Mildred Henderson
Ellen Marie Hicks
Ora Lee Hudson
Clarence Lee Hutchinson
Carl Edward Jackson
Clara Frances Jackson
*Cleon Jenkins
John C. Jenkins
Betty Nadine Johnson
*Annie Pearl Jones

David Jones
Harry Jones, Jr.
Roosevelt Franklin Jones
Bertha Mae Kaphers
Joyce Ann Lightfoot
Mae Alice McCloud
Rudine McCaslin
Marietta McDonald
Clarence Alphonso McGill
*Jimmy Cleveland McKinney
Odell Prince Miles
Robert Costey McKnight
James Croom Miller
Novellia Beatrice Moore
Christine Laressa Neal
Bobbie Ray Nelson
*Roberta Edith Parks
Pearlie Mae Penny
Treatha Mae Murray
Atlene Peoples
Fannie Louise Perry
Charles Plummer
Alice Marie Powers
*Denefield Wesley Player, Jr.
Lizzie Polly Robinson
Margaret Robinson
Laundry Rollins
Katie Mae Rowe
*Bernard Micheal Simmons
*Annese Singleton
Charles Edward Smith
Elaine Carroll Stoney
Beatrice Cornelia Thomas
Karen Frances Toombs
Mary Jane Walker
Doris Cynthia Watson
Effie Lucile Washington
Frank Washington
Barbara Lee Williams
*Josie Mae Williams
Willie Beatrice Williams
*Irvin Victor Woods

*This Student Maintained a General Average of "B".
***This Student Maintained a General Average of "A Minus".

ANNUAL CLASS NIGHT PROGRAM

THURSDAY, MAY 30, 1957

LINCOLN HIGH SCHOOL AUDITORIUM
8:00 P. M.

<u>C A L E N A R</u>

Sunday, May 26, 3:00 P. M.   Annual Sermon

Wednesday, May 29, 10:00 A. M.   Senior Awards Day

Thursday, May 30, 8:00 P. M.   Class Night

P. M.

Friday, May 31, 8:00 P. M.   Commencement Exercises

You are cordially invited to attend all exercises

CLASS NIGHT PROGRAM

PROCESSIONAL

Devotional Period .... Walter Gilespie

Welcome Address ...... Gloria Brooks, Class President

Clarient Solo .... George Gibson Jr.

Class History .... Ellen Hicks

Musical Selection .... Ensemble Senior

Class Prophecy .... Beatrice Thomas

Vocal Solo .... Jacquelyn Curinton

Class Personalities .... Ethel Campbell

Class Poem .... Doris Watson

Cornet Solo .... Irving Woods Jr.

Class Will .... Jeraline Bryant

Musical Selection .... Senior Band Members

Presentation of Key................ Gloria Brooks

Acceptance of Key .... Donald Brown

Announcements

Valedictory .... Randolph Butler

Class Song

Recessional

J U N I O R   E S C O R T S

Gloria Clark   Donald Brown

USHERETTES   USHERS

Jacquelyn Jordan   Samuel Hunter

Bertha Ward ....   Earl Jones

Louise James   James Cato

S P O N S O R S

Mrs. F. M. Jones   Mr. N. B. Rivers

NO. 70 THE WEAVERS

A. QUINN JONES ELEMENTARY SCHOOL'S

Promotional Exercises

MAY 26, 1958

TO

JUNE 5, 1958

AUDITORIUM

CALENDAR OF EVENTS

May 25, Annual Sermon and Graduation of Kindergarten

June 3, Primary Operetta "Goldilock's Adventure"

June 5, Sixth Grade Promotional Exercises

June 5, Closing Day

PROGRAM

Sunday, May 25, 1958—11:00 A.M.

Processional ....Barcarolle

Hymn ....Faith Of Our Fathers

Faith of our fathers living still in spite of danger, fire and sword;
O how our hearts beat high with joy, whene'er we hear that
glorious word.
Faith of our fathers! holy faith! We will be true to thee till death.

Faith of our fathers we will love both friend and foe in all our
strife
And preach thee, too, as love knows how, by kind-ly words
and vir-tous life:
Faith of our fathers! holy faith! We will be true to thee till death.

Invocation

Children Of The Heavenly King ....F. Martin
Chorus

Sermon ....Elder Malchom Phipps
Pastor, Seventh Day Adventist Church
Orlando, Florida

Joshua Fit De Battle of Jericho ....W. Howorth
Chorus

Offertory

Announcements

Presentation of Kindergarten Certificates

All We Can ....Lillenas
Kindergarten

Recessional

Benediction

PROGRAM

Thursday, June 5, 1958 — 1:00 P.M.

Processional ....Pomp and Circumstance

I Would Be True

Responsive Reading

Chant

Hymn of Praise ....Class

Play—"The Rainbow"

COLORS	CHARACTERS
Rainbow	Willie Annette Brown
Yellow	Shirley Knight
Red	Eddie Mae Williams
Green	Carrie Mae Daniels
Purple	Angela Robinson
Blue	Gloria Jean Stanley
	Annette Lauretta Young

Presentation of Certificates

Class Song ....Over The Rainbow

Announcements

Recessional ....School March

SIXTH GRADE CLASS ROLL

Anderson, Shirley
Baines, Catherine
Barnes, Tiney
Bivins, Geneva
Boykins, Leona
Boykins, Obie
Bradley, Joseph
Bradley, Virginia
Brewer, Audrey
Brockington, Nathaniel
Brown, Alfred
Brown, Eugene
Brown, Willine Annette
Buggs, Alton
Campbell, Jesse Lamar, Jr.
Carter, Willie Fred
Cohen, Alphonso
Choen, Leola
Counts, Lendon
Cunningham, Julia Mae
Daniels, Annie Delores
Daniels, Carrie Mae
Davis, Johnnie
Dennard, Johnnie Lee, Jr.
Dickerson, Nellie Lee
Ferguson, Delores
Foreman, Alfred
Foster, Louise
Garvin, Levon

Garvin, Lorenzo C.
Gillislee, Joyce Mae
Goode, Rena Mae
Graham, Joan
Haile, Moses Nathaniel
Hicks, Charles
Hughes, Jeanette
Irving, Nellie Mae
Issac, Carolyn
Jackson, Antoinette Arvette
Jackson, Daniel
James, Lucile
Jenkins Bonnie
Johnson, Claretha
Johnson, Frank
King, Elijah Bell
Knight, Lillie Mae
Knight, Lyra Mae
Knights, Shirley Gwendolyn
Lane, James E.
Lucky, Will Henry
Lyons, Charles
Lyons, Evelyn
Lyons, Willie James
McGlon, Shirley Ann
Miles, Davis
Milligan, Rutha Mae
Nattiel, LaBarbara Lucille
Norman, Alice Mae

Norman, Frank
Patrick, Wayne Allen
Perkins, Dollie Ruth
Perry, Alton Lee
Poole, Laura Lee
Powers, Alvoid
Roberson, Fred
Roberts, Edna Virginia
Robinson, Angela
Scott, Curtis
Sherman, Eddie
Souder, Florida Jean
Spikes, Joseph Henry
Stanley, Gloria Jean
Taylor, Samuel W.
Thomas, Annie Mae
Thomas, Lawrence
Townsend, Frank
Washington, Rutha Mae
Welch, Marvin
White head, Martha
Williams, Celestine
Williams, Cora Elizabeth
Williams, Eddie Mae
Williams, Lila Mae
Williams, Rufus
Woods, Franklin
Young, Annette Lauretta
Young, Frankie Mae

KINDERGARTEN CLASS ROLL   1957-1958

Acosta, Michael Leslie
Anderson, Howard Louis
Banks, Michael Edward
Banks, Wanda Cecelia
Blunt, Lucile
Booker, Sandra LaRue
Brown, Patricia Gay
Brown, Yvette
Cambridge, Janice Lavonca
Bryant, Edith Deloris
Carter, Carliss Yvonne
Carter, Faylene Darnell
Chatman, Charlie James
Clark, Theodore Roosevelt
Davis, Aleatha Eugenia
Davis, Dolly Ann
Day, Tony Curtis
Dexter, James Edward
Duncan, Iris Michelle
Duncan, Sulmarie
Edwards, Cornelia
Ellis, Erthy
Ewell, Colleen Lee

Ferguson, L. Melanthcheon
Gainey, Gloria Jean
George, Faye Claire
Hall, Deborah Elaine
Hightower, Joseph, III.
Holley, Cedric Norvell
Hollis, Ida Nadine
Hyler, Virgin Yvonne
Jones, Charles Bernard
Jones, Teresa Lenora
Lang, Charles Edward
Leath, Charlie Frank
Long, Beatrice Kathie
Lovette, Andrew Windell
Middelton, Sharron Lucile
Milligan, Nathan Bonopart
Mills, Patricia Ann
Moore, Elray
Moore, Kathy
Morris, Raymond Nathaniel
Murray, William, Jr.
Nealey, Sheila Ann
Norman, Ethel Mae

Perkins, James William
Platt, Windell Maurice
Quaintance, Luther Eugene
Robinson, Vida Sue
Sapp, Ronnie Stafford
Shade, Tony Larry
Smith, Mary Deloris
Smith, Roosevelt
Spann, Constance Yvonne
Stephens, Billy Andrew
Taylor, John Ceasar
Taylor, Willie George
Townsend, William Tanner
Usher, Sharon
White, Howard Stanley
Wilkerson, Cynthia Venelia
Williams, Bruce Maurice
Williams, James
Williams, Ricky Eyvonne
Wilson, Deborah Lynne
Young, Aaron Sylvester

VAGA-BOND CLUB INC.

TENTH ANNIVERSARY PROGRAM

MT. PLEASANT M.E. CHURCH

SUNDAY JANUARY 22, 1961

11: OO A. M.

PROGRAMME

ORDER OF SERVICE	REV. FERGUSON, PASTOR
OCCASION	L.V. DAVIS
SOLO	MRS. C.L. MIGKLE, TEACHER LINCOLN HIGH SCHOOL
INTRODUCTION OF SPEAKER	C.W. NORTON, SUPERVISOR OF SCHOOLS, ALACHUA COUNTY
ADDRESS	PROFESSOR A. QUINN JONES RETIRED PRINCIPAL, LINCOLN HIGH SCHOOL
PRESENTATION	J.V. HARPER, PRESIDENT
SELECTION	MISS MARIAM ACOSTA
OFFETORY	DR. E.A. COSBY, DR. C. W. BANKS
REMARKS	REV. FERGUSON, PASTOR
BENEDICTION	

CLUB OFFICERS

1960-61

J.V. HARPER	PRESIDENT
ARNOLD DORSEY	VICE-PRESIDENT
T.J. HARPER	SECRETARY
A .C. CAMBRIDGE	TREASURER
T. COWARD	PARLIAMENTARIAN
L.V. DAVIS	CHAPLAIN

MEMBERS

R.B. AYER	F.E. JENKINS
C.W. BANKS	W.L. JOHNSON
CHAS. CHESTNUT	T.B. McPHERSON
E.A. COSBY	R.M. McGHEE
E. BROWN	B.H. WIMBY
A.L. DANIELS	F.G. WINGATE
E.C. GEORGE	
J. DUNCAN	

TESTIMONIAL DINNER

honoring

Mrs. Frederica M. Jones

and

Mrs. Elizabeth A. Glasper

Retiring Teachers

of

LINCOLN HIGH SCHOOL

Gainesville, Florida

———

Thursday Evening, June 2, 1966

Eight o'clock

Holiday Inn

Gainesville, Florida

MRS. FREDERICA M. JONES

Mrs. Jones has been a teacher in the public schools for 40 years. She taught for two years in the Duval County School system, and thirty-eight years here in Alachua County, as a teacher of English in Lincoln High School.

Mrs. Jones holds membership with the National Council of Teachers of English, Florida Council of Teachers of English, the National Education Association, the American Teachers Association, Florida State Teachers Association, Alachua County Teachers Association, the Department of Classroom Teachers and the Lincoln High School Parents and Teachers Association.

She is a member of Sigma Gamma Rho Sorority and Greater Bethel A.M.E. Church where she serves as organist for the Sunday School and choir No. 3.

She was awarded a Master of Arts degree by Florida A & M University.

She is the wife of Professor A. Quinn Jones Sr., former principal of Lincoln High School, whom she joins in retirement.

MRS. ELIZABETH A. GLASPER

Mrs. Glasper is retiring from a teaching career of 27 years, all in Alachua County, and seventeen years as teacher of English, Junior High Department at Lincoln High School. She has been elected chairman of the English Department by her associates for several years. She is an active member of the Parents and Teachers Association, serving as general chairman of the program planning committee.

Mrs. Glasper holds membership in the National Council of Teachers of English, Florida Council of Teachers of English, the National Education Association, the American Teachers Association, Florida State Teachers Association, Alachua County Teachers Association and the Department of Classroom Teachers.

She is a member of Mt. Carmel Baptist Church and the Ladies' Auxiliary to the American Legion. Mrs. Glasper will be remembered for her speaking ability. She earned her Master of Arts Degree from Columbia University.

Mrs. Glasper is the wife of William Glasper, owner of Air-Way Cleaners of this city, and the mother of a son, Ray.

Programme

Jᴏʜɴ Dᴜᴋᴇs, Jʀ., *Toastmaster*

Invocation..Rev. L. A. Haisley

Occasion..Mrs. Jean W. Brown

Solo—"Somewhere"..Julius V. Harper
Leonard Bernstein

Reading..Nathaniel Clark

Music—"You'll Never Walk Alone"..............Faculty Ensemble
Rodgers and Hammerstein

Tribute..O. W. Nealy, Principal
Lincoln High School

Citations and Presentations

Response..Honorees

Solo—"May the Good Lord Bless and Keep You"
Meredith Willson
Miss Juanita Leverette

Acknowledgement of Guests

Dismissal..Toastmaster

Obsequies
For The Late
Mr. Allen Quinn Jones, Sr.

1:00 P.M.
Saturday, December 6, 1997

Greater Bethel African Methodist Episcopal Church
Gainesville, Florida
Reverend David W. Green, Pastor

Interment
Forest Meadows East Memorial Park
Gainesville, Florida

Arrangements Entrusted
To The Care Of
Chestnut Funeral Home
Gainesville, Florida

Phillips Mortuary
Jacksonville, Florida

Obituary

Allen Quinn Jones, Sr. of Gainesville, Florida died December 2nd, 1997 at Gainesville Health and Rehabilitation Center at the age of 104. Mr. Jones was born March 3, 1893 in Quincy, Florida to the late Joseph Jones and Rosa McDonald Jones.

He received his Bachelors of Science degree from Florida A & M College, Master of Science degree from Hampton Institute. He did further study at New York University toward his doctorate degree.

Mr. Jones was affiliated with the following: Greater Bethel A.M.E. Church, where he served as Superintendant of the Sunday School, and as a trustee. Served as principal of Union Academy and Lincoln High School for thirty-six years, member of Alpha Phi Alpha Fraternity, Inc., member of Prince Hall F.A.A.Y. Masons, member of the local state and national retired teachers associations.

Leaving to rejoice in his memories are: one son, Dr. Oliver H. Jones (Juanita) Gainesville, FL; two daughters, Lydia J. Martin, Ocala, FL, Mrs. Vera J. Rogers (Arnett) Jacksonville, FL; two sisters-in-law, Miss Bernice Cooper, Mrs. Marguerite Rice, Fernandina Beach, FL; several grandchildren, great grandchildren, great great grandchildren; nieces, cousins and many friends.

Order Of Service

Processional

Hymn .... Mass Choir
"When Peace Like A River"

Invocation .... Reverend Geraldine W. McClellan

Scripture .... Reverend Winston J. Bradley
(Favorite Scripture) 1 Corrinthians, Chapter 13

Solo .... Reverend Sandra Bradley

Acknowledgments and
Resolutions .... Sister Madelyn Vallery

Reflections .... Brother Andrew Brown
Class Leader

Hymn .... Mass Choir
"A Mighty Fortress Is Our God"

Eulogy .... Reverend David W. Green

Recessional

Pallbearers
Brothers of
Alpha Phi Alpha Fraternity, Inc.

Flower Attendants
Mass Choir and Ushers

So live, that when thy summons comes to join
The innumberable caravan, which moves
To that mysterious realm, where each shall take
His chamber in the silent halls of death,
Thou go not, like the querry-slave at night,
Scourged to his dungeon, but sustained and soothed
By an unfaltering trust, approach thy grave,
Like one who warps the drapery of his couch
About him, and lies down to pleasant dreams.

William Cullen Bryant

Acknowledgment
Our deepest gratitude is extended to all who expressed
sympathy during our hours of bereavement. May God's
richest blessing be with you.

The Jones Family

UNIVERSITY OF
FLORIDA

George A. Smathers Libraries
Associate Director for Collections

204 Library West
PO Box 117001
Gainesville, FL 32611-7001
(352) 392-0342
Fax: (352) 392-7251
http://www.uflib.ufl.edu

July 22, 2003

Dr. Oliver H. Jones
815 NE 24th Street
Gainesville, Florida 32641

Dear Dr. Jones:

Following discussions with your daughter, Sheryle, I am writing to confirm our
plans for your event to be held Sunday, September 14, 2003 at the Smathers Library
in the University of Florida. The reception and presentation will take place in the
exhibition lobby and the research room of the Department of Special and Area
Studies Collections which is located on the second floor of the Smathers Library. We
have scheduled the event to last between 2 pm and 5 pm. The room will be available
to you before 2 pm for any preliminary set-up that you may require. The Howe
Society, a support group for the Special Collections, is pleased to be a sponsor for
your presentation.

I am grateful for the opportunity to be working with you and Sheryle, and I look
forward to a successful Sunday meeting. Please do not hesitate to call if you have
any questions.

Sincerely,

John E. Ingram
Director for Collections

Copies: Ms. Sheryle Jones

About The Author

A. Quinn Jones was an educational trailblazer for African-Americans in Florida. Born in Quincy, Florida in 1893, he fulfilled his destiny during the segregation era. He earned his B.A. degree from Florida A & M College in 1915 and his M.A. degree from Hampton Institute in 1935. His Objective was to help others attain their goals of academic achievement.

Under his leadership, in 1926 Lincoln High School (Gainesville, Florida) became the second high school in Florida to receive accreditation. He extended the grade levels from 10th thru 12th allowing students to officially earn a diploma. He held the esteemed position of principal until his retirement in 1957. A. Quinn Jones Elementary School (currently the A. Quinn Jones Center) was named in tribute to his untiring commitment to the Gainesville and Alachua County communities.

www.ingramcontent.com/pod-product-compliance
Lightning Source LLC
Chambersburg PA
CBHW020418290526
45785CB00002B/621